Weigh

Freestyle Meal Prep 2019-20

Selected and Most Delicious WW Smart points Recipes to Lose Weight & Transform Your Body - 30 Days Meal Plan – Lose Up to 30 Pounds in 30 Days

By
Autumn Austin

Copyright © **Autumn Austin** 2019

All rights reserved. No part of this publication maybe reproduced, stored or transmitted in any form or by any means, electronic, mechanical, photocopying, recording, scanning, or otherwise without written permission from the author. It is illegal to copy this book, post it to a website, or distribute it by any other means without permission.

Autumn Austin the moral right to be identified as the author of this work.

Table of Contents

Introduction 6
Day 1 7
Day 2 10
Day 3 13
Day 4 16
Day 5 20
Day 6 23
Day 7 27
Day 8 30
Day 9 33
Day 10 36
Day 11 39
Day 12 42
Day 13 45
Day 14 48
Day 15 52
Day 16 55
Day 17 58
Day 18 62
Day 19 65
Day 20 68
Day 21 71
★★ WW Salad, Soup & Snacks ★★ 73
Balsamic Cucumber Salad 73

Mediterranean Chicken Orzo Soup ... 73
Mediterranean Shrimp Orzo Salad ... 74
Favorite Mediterranean Salad ... 75
Greek Spring Soup ... 76
Roasted Red Pepper and Tomato Soup ... 77
Greek Lemon Chicken Soup ... 78
Dad's Greek Salad ... 78
15 Minute Mediterranean Chickpea Salad ... 79
Loaded Mediterranean Hummus ... 79
Crock Pot Chunky Monkey Paleo Trail Mix ... 80
Peanut Butter Banana Greek Yogurt Bowl ... 81
Lemon Chicken Orzo Soup ... 82
Smoky Loaded Eggplant Dip: Baba Ganoush ... 82
Savory Feta Spinach and Sweet Red Pepper Muffins ... 84
Mediterranean Roasted Chickpeas Recipe ... 85
Mediterranean Cobb Salad ... 85
Quinoa Tabbouleh Salad ... 86
Easy Moroccan Chickpea Stew ... 87
★★ WW Fish & Sea food ★★ ... 88
Mediterranean Seafood Stew ... 88
Mediterranean Seafood Sauté with Garlic Couscous ... 89
Zarzuela de Pescado ... 89
Mediterranean Fish (Flounder) ... 91
Easy Mediterranean Fish Skillet ... 92
Mediterranean Baked Fish ... 93

Pan-Roasted Fish with Mediterranean Tomato Sauce 93

★★WW Desserts ★★ 95

Mint Chocolate Chip Ice Cream 95

Italian Apple Olive Oil Cake 95

Lavender honey ice cream 97

Paleo Raspberry Cream Pies (vegan, grain-free, gluten-free, dairy-free) 97

Chocolate Avocado Pudding With Hazelnuts And Sea Salt 99

No-Bake Mint Chip Cookies 99

Grain-Free Hummingbird Cake 100

Maple Vanilla Bean Meringue Cookies 101

Vegan Mango Mousse 102

Blackberry Frozen Yogurt 103

Conclusion 104

Introduction

During the modern world The Weight Watchers Program is one of the most effective and popular weight loss plans for those who require to lose weight. Weight Watchers is becoming popular day by day because it attracts hundreds of thousands of new members every year. This program is flexible, points-based system appeals to many dieters and stresses the importance of living a healthy lifestyle.

If you're looking for an evidence-based weight-loss program, you can choose Weight Watchers. Because, studies have found that Weight Watchers is an effective way to lose weight and keep it off and it lets you indulge in your favorite foods once in a while, Weight Watchers might help you reach your health and wellness goals. Weight Watchers offers many resources for their members. From recipes to tips and advice, members can find information on how to diet and stay healthy at the same time.

Day 1

BREAKFAST

Mediterranean Eggs

Prep Time 5 mins, Cook Time 1 hr 18 mins, Servings: 6

Ingredients

- 4-5 small or 1 1/2 large yellow onions halved and sliced
- 1 tablespoon butter
- 1 tablespoon extra virgin olive oil
- 1 clove garlic minced
- 1/3 cup firmly packed julienne cut sun dried tomatoes
- 6-8 large eggs
- 3 ounces crumbled feta cheese
- Coarse kosher salt and freshly ground black pepper
- Parsley optional, finely chopped
- Ciabatta rolls optional

Instructions

- In a large cast iron or stainless steel skillet, heat butter and oil over medium heat. Once the butter is melted add the onions to the pan and stir gently to coat in the butter and oil, arranging them in an even layer. Reduce the heat so the onions just barely sizzle. Allow the onions to cook, stirring every 5 to 10 minutes, until they are soft and a deep brown color, about one hour.
- Add garlic and sun dried tomatoes and cook, stirring, for about 1-3 minutes or until fragrant. Arrange the mixture in an even layer in the pan, then carefully crack eggs over the top. Sprinkle with crumbled feta, salt, and pepper. Cover with a tight fitting lid and allow to cook undisturbed for 10-15 minutes. Watch the eggs carefully in the last few minutes as the yolks change quickly. You can check yolk doneness by jiggling the pan. Runny yolks will jiggle slightly while firm yolks shouldn't move at all.
- Remove pan from the heat and sprinkle with chopped parsley if desired. Serve on crusty ciabatta rolls.

Nutritional info per serving : Calories 183 , Calories from Fat 99 , Total Fat 11g 17% , Saturated Fat 5g 25% , Cholesterol 181mg 60%, Points Value: 10

LUNCH

Spinach & Egg Scramble with Raspberries

Prep/Cook 10 m, 1 serving

Ingredients

- 1 teaspoon canola oil
- 1½ cups baby spinach (1½ ounces)
- 2 large eggs, lightly beaten
- Pinch of kosher salt
- Pinch of ground pepper
- 1 slice whole-grain bread, toasted
- ½ cup fresh raspberries

Instructions

- Heat oil in a small nonstick skillet over medium-high heat. Add spinach and cook until wilted, stirring often, 1 to 2 minutes.
- Transfer the spinach to a plate. Wipe the pan clean, place over medium heat and add eggs.
- Cook, stirring once or twice to ensure even cooking, until just set, 1 to 2 minutes.
- Stir in the spinach, salt and pepper. Serve the scramble with toast and raspberries.

Nutritional info per serving : 296 calories; 16 g fat(4 g sat); 7 g fiber; 21 g carbohydrates; 18 g protein; 79 mcg, Points Value: 8

DINNER

Quinoa Falafel

Prep Time 10 mins, Cook Time 20 mins, Servings: 2

Ingredients

- 1 Cup Cooked Quinoa
- 1/2 Cup Cooked Garbanzo Beans
- 1-2 Cloves Garlic
- 1/4 Grated Carrot
- 2 Tbsp. Chopped Parsley
- 1 Tbsp. Chopped Mint
- 1 tsp. Lemon Zest
- 1 tsp. Ground Cumin
- 1 Tbsp. Chopped Onion
- 1 tsp. Tahini
- 1/4 tsp. Smoked Paprika

- Sea salt and Black Pepper to taste
- 1 lemon juiced
- 1 tablespoon tahini
- 3 cloves garlic minced
- 1/4 teaspoon smoked paprika
- salt and pepper to taste

Yogurt Tahini Sauce

- 1/2 plain yogurt

Instructions

- Combine all the falafel ingredients in a food processor and purée until the mixture forms a ball in the machine. You want the mix to form a 'dough', but be careful not to over-mix it, as that will make it too sticky. Taste and adjust seasoning.
- Measure out dough into approximately 1 Tbsp. sized balls. Set a frying pan to medium heat. One the pan is warm, add enough high-heat suitable oil (such as avocado or coconut) to cover the bottom of the pan. Add falafel, a few at a time as to not crowd the pan. Let brown on all sides - I found the best way to do this was with a slight agitation of the pan. Serve with fresh veggies of choice and Yoghurt Tahini Sauce.
- Wraps, sprouts, avocado, cucumber, peppers, greens, mint, hummus, olives, or tomatoes to serve.

Yogurt Tahini Sauce

- Combine all ingredients in a bowl. Taste and adjust for seasoning.

Nutritional info per serving : Calories 145 , Calories from Fat 36 , Total Fat 4g 6% , Sodium 18mg 1% , Potassium 298mg 9% , Total Carbohydrates 22g 7%, Points Value: 5

Day 2

BREAKFAST

Mediterranean Feta & Quinoa Egg Muffins

Prep Time: 15 mins, Cook Time: 30 mins, Servings: 12 muffins

Ingredients

- 2 cups baby spinach finely chopped
- 1/2 cup finely chopped onion*
- 1 cup chopped or sliced tomatoes {cherry or grape tomatoes work well}
- 1/2 cup chopped {pitted} kalamata olives
- 1 tablespoon chopped fresh oregano
- 2 teaspoons high oleic sunflower oil plus optional extra for greasing muffin tins
- 8 eggs
- 1 cup cooked quinoa*
- 1 cup crumbled feta cheese
- 1/4 teaspoon salt

Instructions

- Pre-heat oven to 350 degrees fahrenheit, and prepare 12 silicone muffin holders on a baking sheet, or grease a 12 cup muffin tin with oil and set aside.
- Chop vegetables and heat a skillet to medium. Add vegetable oil and onions and saute for 2 minutes. Add tomatoes and saute for another minute, then add spinach and saute until wilted, about 1 minute. Turn off heat and stir in olives and oregano, and set aside.
- Place eggs in a blender or mixing bowl and blend/mix until well combined. Pour eggs into a mixing bowl {if using a blender} then add quinoa, feta cheese, veggie mixture, and salt, and stir until well combined.
- Pour mixture in to silicone cups or greased muffin tins, dividing equally, and bake in oven for 30 minutes, or until eggs have set and muffins are a light golden brown. Allow to cool for 5 minutes before serving, or may be chilled and eaten cold, or re-heated in a microwave the next day.

Notes

- Omit onions for a Low FODMAP option.

- If you have precooked quinoa in your fridge, it works perfectly in this recipe, but if you are cooking it specifically for this recipe I recommend making a big batch {2 cups water per each cup of dry, rinsed quinoa} and saving the extra for leftovers.

Nutritional info per serving : Calories: 113kcal, Carbohydrates: 5g, Protein: 6g, Fat: 7g, Points Value: 6

LUNCH

Meal-Prep Falafel Bowls with Tahini Sauce

Prep/Cook Time: 20 m , 4 servings

Ingredients

- 1 (8 ounce) package frozen prepared falafel
- ⅔ cup water
- ½ cup whole-wheat couscous
- 1 (16 ounce) bag steam-in-bag fresh green beans
- ½ cup Tahini Sauce (see associated recipe)
- ¼ cup pitted Kalamata olives
- ¼ cup crumbled feta cheese

Instructions

- Prepare falafel according to package Instructions; set aside to cool.
- Bring water to a boil in a small saucepan. Stir in couscous, cover and remove from heat. Allow to stand until the liquid is absorbed, about 5 minutes. Fluff with a fork; set aside.
- Prepare green beans according to package Instructions. Prepare Tahini Sauce. Divide among 4 small condiment containers with lids and refrigerate.
- Divide the green beans among 4 single-serving containers with lids.
- Top each with ½ cup couscous, one-fourth of the falafel and 1 tablespoon each olives and feta.
- Seal and refrigerate for up to 4 days. To serve, reheat in the microwave until heated through, about 2 minutes.
- Dress with tahini sauce just before eating.

To make ahead: Prepare through Step 5; refrigerate sealed containers for up to 4 days. Reheat as directed in Step 6.

Nutritional info per serving : 500 calories; 27 g fat(5 g sat); 11 g fiber; 55 g carbohydrates; 15 g protein; 53 mcg, Points Value: 20

DINNER

Mediterranean Chicken Orzo Soup

Prep: 20 min. Cook: 25 min, 6 servings (2-1/2 quarts)

Ingredients

- 2 tablespoons olive oil, divided
- 3/4 pound boneless skinless chicken breasts, cubed
- 2 celery ribs, chopped
- 2 medium carrots, chopped
- 1 small onion, chopped
- 1/2 teaspoon salt
- 1/2 teaspoon dried oregano
- 1/4 teaspoon pepper
- 1/4 cup white wine or additional reduced-sodium chicken broth
- 1 carton (32 ounces) reduced-sodium chicken broth
- 1 teaspoon minced fresh rosemary
- 1 bay leaf
- 1 cup uncooked whole wheat orzo pasta
- 1 teaspoon grated lemon zest
- 1 tablespoon lemon juice
- Minced fresh parsley, optional

Instructions

- In a large saucepan, heat 1 tablespoon oil over medium-high heat. Add chicken; cook and stir 6-8 minutes or until no longer pink. Remove from pan.
- In same pan, heat remaining oil over medium-high heat. Add vegetables, salt, oregano and pepper; cook and stir 4-6 minutes or until vegetables are crisp-tender. Add wine, stirring to loosen browned bits from pan. Stir in broth, rosemary and bay leaf; bring to a boil.
- Add orzo. Reduce heat; simmer, covered, 15-18 minutes or until orzo is tender, stirring occasionally. Return chicken to pan; heat through. Stir in lemon zest and juice; remove bay leaf. If desired, top each serving with parsley.

Nutritional info per serving : 1-2/3 cups: 223 calories, 6g fat (1g saturated fat), 31mg cholesterol, 630mg sodium, 23g carbohydrate (2g sugars, 5g fiber), 17g protein, Points Value: 20

Day 3

BREAKFAST

Mediterranean Egg White Breakfast Sandwich

Prep Time: 5 mins, Cook Time: 25 mins

Ingredients

- 1 teaspoon butter
- ¼ cup egg whites
- Salt and pepper to taste
- 1 teaspoon chopped fresh herbs such as parsley, basil, rosemary
- 1 whole grain seeded ciabatta roll
- 1 tablespoon pesto
- 1-2 slices muenster cheese (or other cheese such as provolone, Monterey Jack, etc.)
- About ½ cup roasted tomatoes (recipe below)

Roasted Tomatoes:

- 10 ounces grape tomatoes
- 1 tablespoon extra virgin olive oil
- Kosher salt and coarse black pepper to taste

Instructions

- Melt butter over medium heat in a small nonstick skillet. Pour in egg whites and season with salt and pepper. Sprinkle with fresh herbs. Cook for 3-4 minutes or until egg is done, flipping once.
- Meanwhile, toast ciabatta bread in toaster. Spread both halves with pesto when done. Place the egg on bottom half of sandwich roll, folding if necessary, then top with cheese. Add roasted tomatoes and top half of roll. 1 sandwich.
- To make the roasted tomatoes: Preheat oven to 400 degrees. Slice tomatoes in half lengthwise. Place on a baking sheet and drizzle with the olive oil. Toss to coat. Season with salt and pepper and roast in oven for about 20 minutes. Skins will appear wrinkled when done.

Nutritional info per serving : Serving size: 1 Calories: 458, Fat: 24g, Saturated fat: 8g, Protein: 21g. Cholesterol: 30g , Points Value: 20

LUNCH

Garden-Fresh Omelets

Prep/Cook 35 m, 4 servings

Ingredients

- 1⅓ cups coarsely chopped tomatoes, drained
- 1 cup coarsely chopped, seeded cucumber
- ½ of a ripe avocado, halved, seeded, peeled and chopped
- ½ cup coarsely chopped red onion (1 medium)
- 1 clove garlic, minced
- 2 tablespoons snipped fresh parsley
- 2 tablespoons red wine vinegar
- 1 tablespoon olive oi

- 2 eggs
- 1½ cups refrigerated or frozen egg product, thawed
- ¼ cup water
- 1 tablespoon snipped fresh oregano or 1 teaspoon dried oregano, crushed
- ¼ teaspoon salt
- ¼ teaspoon ground black pepper
- ⅛ teaspoon crushed red pepper
- ¼ cup crumbled reduced-fat feta cheese

Instructions

- For salsa, in a medium bowl stir together tomatoes, cucumber, avocado, onion, garlic, parsley, vinegar and 1 teaspoon of the oil. Set aside (see Tip). In a medium bowl, whisk together eggs, egg product, the water, oregano, salt, black pepper and crushed red pepper. For each omelet, in an 8-inch nonstick skillet heat ½ teaspoon of the remaining oil over medium heat. Add ½ cup of the egg mixture to skillet. Stir eggs with a spatula until mixture resembles cooked egg pieces surrounded by liquid. Stop stirring, but continue cooking until egg is set. Spoon ⅓ cup of the salsa over one side of the cooked egg mixture. Remove from skillet; fold omelet over the filling. Repeat to make four omelets total. Serve each omelet with one-fourth of the remaining salsa. Sprinkle each omelet with 1 tablespoon of the feta cheese.
- To make ahead: If desired, make the salsa ahead and cover and chill it for up to 8 hours.

Nutritional info per serving : Serving size: 1 omelet, about ¾ cup salsa and 1 tablespoon reduced-fat feta cheese , 201 calories; 12 g fat(3 g sat); 2 g fiber; 9 g carbohydrates; 15 g protein; 43 mcg, Points Value: 6

DINNER

Quinoa Bowls with Roasted Red Pepper Sauce

Prep Time: 15 mins, Cook Time: 5 mins, Serves 8

Ingredients

Roasted Red Pepper Sauce:

- 1 16 ounce jar roasted red peppers, drained (or roast your own red peppers and win the food game!)
- 1 clove garlic
- 1/2 teaspoon salt (more to taste)
- juice of one lemon
- 1/2 cup olive oil
- 1/2 cup almonds
- For the Mediterranean Bowls (build your own bowls based on what you like)
- cooked quinoa
- spinach, kale, or cucumber
- feta cheese
- kalamata olives
- pepperoncini
- thinly sliced red onion
- hummus
- fresh basil or parsley
- olive oil, lemon juice, salt, pepper

Instructions

Pulse all the ingredients for the sauce in a food processor or blender until mostly smooth. The texture should be thick and textured (see picture).

- Cook the quinoa according to package Instructions (I always do mine in a rice cooker while I get everything else ready). When the quinoa is done, build yourself a Mediterranean Quinoa Bowl!
- Store leftovers in separate containers and assemble each bowl just before serving, especially the greens and the sauces, as those will get soggy when stored with all the other ingredients.

Nutritional info per serving : Calories Per Serving: 381 , 39% Total Fat 25.6g , 4% Cholesterol 12.6mg , 22% Protein 10.9g, Points Value: 26

Day 4

BREAKFAST

Low-Carb Baked Eggs with Avocado and Feta

Prep Time: 25 minutes, Cook Time: 12-15 minutes, 2 servings

Ingredients

- 4 eggs
- 1 large avocado
- olive oil or non-stick spray for gratin dishes
- 2-3 T crumbled Feta Cheese
- salt and fresh-ground black pepper to taste

Instructions

- Break eggs into individual ramekins and let the eggs and avocado come to room temperature for 15 minutes.
- When the oven comes to temperature, put the gratin dishes on a baking sheet and heat them in the oven for 10 minutes.
- After 15 minutes, peel the avocado and cut each half into 6 slices.
- Remove gratin dishes from the oven and spray with olive oil or non-stick spray.
- Arrange the sliced avocados in each dish and VERY CAREFULLY tip two eggs into each dish.
- Sprinkle with crumbled Feta and season to taste with salt and fresh-ground black pepper. (Remember that Feta is salty; we didn't use much salt.)
- Bake 12-15 minutes, or until the whites are set and the egg yolks are done to your liking.
- Serve hot This is great with Green Tabasco Sauce to add at the table.
- It can be served with whole wheat toast for a low-glycemic breakfast if you don't mind having a few more carbs.

Nutritional info per serving : Calories 304.3, Points Value: 9

LUNCH

Herb-Lovers Lemony Orzo Salad

Prep Time: 15 mins, Cook Time: 15 mins

Ingredients:

- 12 ounces uncooked orzo (or any pasta shape)
- 2 large handfuls fresh baby spinach, chopped
- 1 (15-ounce) can chickpeas (garbanzo beans), rinsed and drained
- 1 English cucumber, diced
- half a small red onion, diced
- 1 cup roughly-chopped fresh basil leaves
- 1 cup roughly-chopped fresh mint leaves
- 1-2 lemons, zested and juiced
- 1/4 cup olive oil
- sea salt and freshly-cracked black pepper, to taste
- optional: 1/2 cup crumbled feta or goat cheese

Instructions:

- Cook the pasta in a large stockpot of generously-salted water until al dente, according to package instructions. Drain pasta then rinse thoroughly in a strainer with cold water until the pasta is chilled. Transfer pasta to a large mixing bowl.
- Add the remaining ingredients to the mixing bowl (using cheese if desired). Toss until evenly combined. Taste, and season with a few generous pinches of salt and pepper, to taste. (I used about 1 teaspoon each of salt and pepper.) Also feel free to add in extra lemon juice if you'd like an extra-lemony salad. (<– My fave.)
- Serve immediately. Or cover and refrigerate for up to 3 days.

Nutritional info per serving : Calories 338, Points Value: 10

DINNER

Baked Falafel Burgers

Prep Time 20 minutes, Cook Time 40 minutes

Ingredients

- 1 bundle fresh parsley (1 bundle yields ~2 cups chopped)
- 3 large cloves garlic
- 1 large lemon (1 large lemon yields ~2 1/2 Tbsp juice)
- 1/2 scant tsp each sea salt + black pepper
- 1 1/4 tsp cumin
- 1 15-ounce can chickpeas (well rinsed and drained)
- 1/4 - 1/2 cup ground raw walnuts, pecans, almonds, or GF oat flour

TOPPINGS / FOR SERVING (optional)

- Garlic Dill sauce
- Chili Garlic Sauce or Sriracha
- 5-minute Hummus
- Tomato
- Lettuce
- Onion
- Pita or sturdy greens (such as chard or collard greens)

Instructions

- Add parsley, garlic, lemon juice, cumin, and a healthy pinch each salt and pepper to a food processor and mix to combine.
- Add chickpeas and pulse until incorporated but still slightly chunky. You want to maintain a bit of texture.
- Transfer to a mixing bowl and add nut meal (or oat flour) and mix again until a loose dough is formed that's firm enough to be handled. Taste and adjust seasonings as needed. I added a touch more salt.
- Draw an "x" in the dough to form 4 sections adjust if altering batch size, then use your hands to form into 4 large patties, adjust if altering batch size roughly 1/2-inch thick.
- Place on a foil-lined baking sheet and refrigerate or freeze for 15 minutes to firm up. Preheat oven to 375 degrees F (in the meantime.
- OPTIONAL STEP: For a little extra crust on the outside, before baking heat a large skillet over medium to medium-high heat and add 2 Tbsp olive or avocado oil. Swirl to coat pan, then add falafel. Carefully flip once golden brown – about 3-4 minutes - and then cook on the other side until golden brown as well - 3-4 more minutes. Return to baking sheet to

- continue baking. Otherwise, just add them straight to the oven for baking.
  o Bake for a total of 30-40 minutes, flipping once at the halfway point for even cooking. The longer you bake them, the firmer they'll get!
  o Serve warm wrapped in a pita or chard bun and desired sauces / toppings. Alternatively, serve atop a salad and use the garlic sauce as a dressing.
  o Burgers will store in the fridge, layered with parchment paper in an airtight container, for several days. Freeze to keep longer.

Nutritional info per serving : Nutrition Per Serving (1 of 4 burgers) , Calories: 180 Fat: 10g Saturated fat: 0.7g Sodium: 620mg Carbohydrates: 17.2g Fiber: 4.6g Sugar: 0.8g Protein: 9.4g , Points Value: 9

Day 5

BREAKFAST

Greek Yogurt Pancakes

Prep Time 15 mins, Cook Time 15 mins, Servings: 6

Ingredients

- 1 1/4 cup all-purpose flour
- 1/4 teaspoon salt
- 2 teaspoons baking powder
- 1 teaspoon baking soda
- 1/4 cup sugar
- 3 tablespoons butter unsalted, melted
- 3 eggs
- 1 1/2 cups Greek yogurt plain, non-fat
- 1/2 cup milk
- 1/2 cup blueberries optional

Instructions

- In a large bowl, whisk flour, salt, baking powder and baking soda.
- In a separate bowl, whisk together sugar, butter, eggs, Greek yogurt, and milk until smooth.
- Add Greek yogurt mixture from step to the flour mixture in step 1 and mix to combine. I like to let batter sit for 20 minutes to get really smooth textured. (optional: fold in blueberries in pancake batter or in half of pancake batter).
- Heat pancake griddle, spray with non-stick butter spray or just brush the griddle with real butter. Pour batter, in 1/4 cupful's, onto the griddle. Cook until the bubbles on top burst and create small holes. Lift up the corners of each pancake to check that it's golden browned on the bottom. Using a wide spatula, flip the pancake and cook it on the other side until lightly browned. Remove pancakes from the griddle onto the warming plate until ready to serve.
- To serve, top each portion of pancakes with a scoop of Greek yogurt and mixed berries (blueberries, raspberries, blackberries).

Nutritional info per serving : Calories 258 , Calories from Fat 72 , Total Fat 8g 12% , Saturated Fat 4g 20% , Cholesterol 101mg 34% , Sodium 389mg 16 , Points Value: 10

LUNCH

Mediterranean Lentil Salad

Prep time 10 mins, Cook time 20 mins, Serves: 4-6

Ingredients

- 1 cup French lentils
- 1 bay leaf
- ¼ cup finely chopped red onion (for a milder taste, you can do 2 chopped green onions instead)
- 3 radishes, quartered and sliced
- 2 celery stalks, chopped
- ½ red bell pepper, chopped
- ¼ cup chopped flat leaf parsley
- Feta (as much or as little as you want)
- 3 tablespoons lemon juice
- 1 tablespoon olive oil
- 1 garlic clove, minced
- ¼-1/2 teaspoon salt, or to taste

Instructions

- Add the lentils and bay leaf to a pot with water covering them by 3 inches. Bring to a boil and reduce to a simmer, cooking uncovered for 15-20 minutes, or until al dente (but not mushy). Once the lentils are done, drain and set aside to cool.
- Meanwhile, add the vegetables (onion through parsley) to a mixing bowl. Make the dressing by combining the lemon juice, olive oil, garlic, and salt in a jar or small bowl.
- Once the lentils have cooled, combine them with the vegetables and toss with the dressing. Mix in desired amount of feta. Taste and adjust seasonings if necessary.
- Leftovers will keep fresh in the fridge for several days.

Nutritional info per serving : Calories: 240.0 , Dietary Fiber: 4.7 g , Sugars: 0.2 g , Total Fat: 17.2 g, Points Value: 8

DINNER

Greek Butter Crescents

Prep: 45 min. Bake: 15 min./batch + cooling, Serving: 5 dozen

Ingredients

- 1 pound butter, melted and cooled
- 3-1/2 cups confectioners' sugar, divided
- 1 large egg yolk
- 1 teaspoon vanilla extract
- 6 cups all-purpose flour
- 1/4 teaspoon baking powder

Instructions

- Preheat oven to 400°. In a large bowl, beat butter and 1/2 cup confectioners' sugar until blended. Beat in egg yolk and vanilla. In another bowl, whisk flour and baking powder; gradually stir into creamed mixture until blended (mixture will be crumbly). Shape heaping tablespoons of dough into crescents. Place 1 in. apart on ungreased baking sheets. Bake 12-15 minutes or until edges are lightly browned. Remove from pans to wire racks to cool 15 minutes.
- Place remaining sugar in a small bowl. Toss slightly cooled cookies in sugar; return cookies to wire rack to cool completely. Toss cookies in sugar once more before serving. Store in an airtight container, adding any remaining confectioners' sugar to cover cookies.

Day 6

BREAKFAST

Avocado Tomato Gouda Socca Pizza {Grain & Egg Free}

Prep Time: 20 mins, Cook Time: 20 mins , Servings : 2

Ingredients :

For the Socca Pizza Crust:

- 1 1/4 cup chickpea/garbanzo bean flour (see notes for brands)
- 1 1/4 cup cold water
- 1/4 tsp sea salt and pepper each (to taste)
- 2 tbsp olive or avocado oil (1 tbsp for heating pan)
- 1 tsp minced Garlic (2 cloves)
- 1 tsp of Onion powder or any other herbed seasoning of choice (optional). You can also use dried herbs here.
- 10 to 12 inch Pan to heat in oven (cast iron works great. See notes for size)

Socca Pizza Toppings:

- 1 Roma tomato sliced
- 1/2 avocado
- 2 oz Gouda (sliced thin). Goats milk Gouda works too. See notes for vegan option.
- 1/4 to 1/3 cup Tomato sauce
- 2-3 tbsp chopped green onion/scallion
- Sprouted greens (onion greens, kale, or broccoli) to top
- Extra Salt/pepper to sprinkle on top
- Red pepper flakes

Instructions

- First Mix your flour, 2 tbsp olive oil, water, and herbs/seasoning together. Whisk until smooth. It's best to let it sit for 15-20 minutes at room temperature.
- While the batter is sitting, preheat oven to broil. Place your pan in the oven to heat for 10 minutes.
- While the pan is preheating, chop/slice your vegetables. Set aside.
- Using oven mitts, remove pan after 10 minutes.
- Add 1 tbsp of oil to the pan and swirl it around to coat pan

- Gently pour in your chickpea/socca batter. Tilt pan so the batter fills and is even. (see notes on pan size)
- Turn oven down to 425F and place pan back in oven for 5- 8 minutes or so. Just until the batter is set. If you are using a bigger pan, the pizza will be thinner and will probably bake faster, so check at 5 minutes.
- Remove from oven.
- Spread the tomato sauce on top. Then add your sliced tomato and avocado. Place your gouda slices on top of the tomato and avocado. Green onion can go on the top or you can wait to add in fresh last.
- Place back in oven for 10-15 minutes until cheese is melted and the socca bread is crispy and brown on outside.
- Remove from the oven. You should be able to slide the pizza crust onto a stone or heat safe surface.
- Add a bunch of sprouts/microgreens on top then any additional toppings. Like more onion, alt/pepper to taste, and red pepper flakes.
- Drizzle olive oil on top. Slice and serve.

Nutritional info per serving : Serving Size: 1/2 recipe Calories: 416, Sugar: 6.8g Sodium: 257mg, Fat: 24.5g, Saturated Fat: 4.7g, Carbohydrates: 36.6g, Fiber: 9.6g, Protein: 15.4g Cholesterol: 9mg , Points Value: 22

LUNCH

Greek Turkey Meatball Gyro with Tzatziki

Prep Time: 10 mins Cook Time: 16 mins, Servings : 4 gyros

Ingredients

Turkey Meatball:

- 1 lb. ground turkey
- 1/4 cup finely diced red onion
- 2 garlic cloves, minced
- 1 teaspoon oregano
- 1 cup chopped fresh spinach
- salt & pepper to season
- 2 tablespoons olive oil

Tzatziki Sauce:

- 1/2 cup plain greek yogurt
- 1/4 cup grated cucumber
- 2 tablespoons lemon juice
- 1/2 teaspoon dry dill
- 1/2 teaspoon garlic powder
- salt to taste
- 1/2 cup thinly sliced red onion
- 1 cup diced tomato

- 1 cup diced cucumber
- 4 whole wheat flatbreads

Instructions

- To a large bowl add, ground turkey, diced red onion, minced garlic, oregano, fresh spinach, salt, and pepper. Using your hands mix all the ingredients together until meat forms a ball and sticks together.
- Then using your hands, form meat mixture into 1" balls. (you should be able to get about 12 meatballs).
- Heat a large skillet to medium high heat. Add olive oil to the pan, and then add the meatballs. Cook each side for 3-4 minutes until they are browned on all sides. Remove from the pan and let rest.
- In the meantime, to a small bowl add greek yogurt, grated cucumber, lemon juice, dill, garlic powder, and salt to taste. Mix together until everything is combined.
- Assemble the gyros: to a flatbread (I like to warm mine up so they are more pliable) add 3 meatballs, sliced red onion, tomato, and cucumber. Then top with Tzatziki sauce.

Nutritional info per serving : Serving Size: 1 flatbread + 3 meatballs , Calories: 429 , Sugar: 4 g , Sodium: 630 mg, Points Value: 13

DINNER

Greek Garlic Chicken

Prep: 20 min. Cook: 3-1/2 hours, 6 servings

Ingredients

- 1/2 cup chopped onion
- 1 tablespoon plus 1 teaspoon olive oil, divided
- 3 tablespoons minced garlic
- 2-1/2 cups chicken broth, divided
- 1/4 cup pitted Greek olives, chopped
- 3 tablespoons chopped sun-dried tomatoes (not packed in oil)
- 1 tablespoon quick-cooking tapioca
- 2 teaspoons grated lemon zest
- 1 teaspoon dried oregano
- 6 boneless skinless chicken breast halves (6 ounces each)
- 1-3/4 cups uncooked couscous

- 1/2 cup crumbled feta cheese

Instructions

- In a small skillet, saute onion in 1 tablespoon oil until crisp-tender. Add garlic; cook 1 minute longer.
- Transfer to a 5-qt. slow cooker. Stir in 3/4 cup broth, olives, tomatoes, tapioca, lemon zest and oregano. Add chicken. Cover and cook on low for 3-1/2-4 hours or until chicken is tender. If desired, cut chicken into pieces.
- In a large saucepan, bring remaining oil and broth to a boil. Stir in couscous. Cover and remove from the heat; let stand for 5 minutes or until broth is absorbed. Serve with chicken; sprinkle with feta cheese.

Nutritional info per serving : 5 ounces cooked chicken with 1/4 cup sauce and 3/4 cup couscous: 475 calories, 11g fat (3g saturated fat), 101mg cholesterol, 683mg sodium, 48g carbohydrate (3g sugars, 3g fiber), 44g protein. , Points Value: 18

Day 7

BREAKFAST

Mediterranean Breakfast Sandwiches

Prep 5 m, Cook Time 20 m, 4 servings

Ingredients

- 4 multigrain sandwich thins
- 4 teaspoons olive oil
- 1 tablespoon snipped fresh rosemary or ½ teaspoon dried rosemary, crushed
- 4 eggs
- 2 cups fresh baby spinach leaves
- 1 medium tomato, cut into 8 thin slices
- 4 tablespoons reduced-fat feta cheese
- ⅛ teaspoon kosher salt
- Freshly ground black pepper

Instructions

- Preheat oven to 375°F. Split sandwich thins; brush cut sides with 2 teaspoons of the olive oil. Place on baking sheet; toast in oven about 5 minutes or until edges are light brown and crisp. Meanwhile, in a large skillet heat the remaining 2 teaspoons olive oil and the rosemary over medium-high heat. Break eggs, one at a time, into skillet. Cook about 1 minute or until whites are set but yolks are still runny. Break yolks with spatula. Flip eggs; cook on other side until done. Remove from heat. Place the bottom halves of the toasted sandwich thins on four serving plates. Divide spinach among sandwich thins on plates. Top each with two of the tomato slices, an egg and 1 tablespoon of the feta cheese. Sprinkle with the salt and pepper. Top with the remaining sandwich thin halves.

Nutritional info per serving : Per serving: 242 calories; 12 g fat(3 g sat); 13 g protein , Points Value: 9

LUNCH

Quinoa Bowls with Roasted Red Pepper Sauce

Prep Time: 15 mins, Cook Time: 5 mins, Serves 8

Ingredients

Roasted Red Pepper Sauce:

- 1 16 ounce jar roasted red peppers, drained (or roast your own red peppers and win the food game!)
- 1 clove garlic
- 1/2 teaspoon salt (more to taste)
- juice of one lemon
- 1/2 cup olive oil
- 1/2 cup almonds

For the Mediterranean Bowls (build your own bowls based on what you like)

- cooked quinoa
- spinach, kale, or cucumber
- feta cheese
- kalamata olives
- pepperoncini
- thinly sliced red onion
- hummus
- fresh basil or parsley
- olive oil, lemon juice, salt, pepper

Instructions

- Pulse all the ingredients for the sauce in a food processor or blender until mostly smooth. The texture should be thick and textured (see picture).
- Cook the quinoa according to package Instructions (I always do mine in a rice cooker while I get everything else ready). When the quinoa is done, build yourself a Mediterranean Quinoa Bowl!
- Store leftovers in separate containers and assemble each bowl just before serving, especially the greens and the sauces, as those will get soggy when stored with all the other ingredients.

Nutritional info per serving : Calories Per Serving: 381 , 39% Total Fat 25.6g , 4% Cholesterol 12.6mg , 22% Protein 10.9g, Points Value: 17

DINNER

Slow-Cooked Moroccan Chicken

Prep: 20 min. Cook: 6 hours, 4 servings

Ingredients

- 4 medium carrots, sliced
- 2 large onions, halved and sliced
- 1 broiler/fryer chicken (3 to 4 pounds), cut up, skin removed
- 1/2 teaspoon salt
- 1/2 cup chopped dried apricots
- 1/2 cup raisins
- 1 can (14-1/2 ounces) reduced-sodium chicken broth
- 1/4 cup tomato paste
- 2 tablespoons all-purpose flour
- 2 tablespoons lemon juice
- 2 garlic cloves, minced
- 1-1/2 teaspoons ground ginger
- 1-1/2 teaspoons ground cumin
- 1 teaspoon ground cinnamon
- 3/4 teaspoon pepper
- Hot cooked couscous

Instructions

- Place carrots and onions in a greased 5-qt. slow cooker. Sprinkle chicken with salt; add to slow cooker. Top with apricots and raisins. In a small bowl, whisk broth, tomato paste, flour, lemon juice, garlic and seasonings until blended; add to slow cooker.
- Cook, covered, on low until chicken is tender, 6-7 hours. Serve with hot cooked couscous.

Nutritional info per serving :1 serving: 435 calories, 9g fat (3g saturated fat), 110mg cholesterol, 755mg sodium, 47g carbohydrate (27g sugars, 6g fiber), 42g protein. , Points Value: 15

Day 8

BREAKFAST

Feta Frozen Yogurt

Prep Time 5 minutes, Freezing Time 4 hours, Servings 3

Ingredients

- 1 cup plain Greek yogurt 200 g
- 1/2 cup feta cheese 50 g
- 1 Tbsp honey 15 mL

Instructions

- Freeze: In a food processor or blender, combine all ingredients until smooth. Pour into a wide dish (it shouldn't be a very thick layer) and freeze until solid.
- Blend: Break frozen mixture into chunks and add back into your blender, along with a few tablespoons of water or milk. Blitz until smooth and creamy, scraping down the sides as needed to get everything blended. Serve drizzled with honey.

Nutritional info per serving : Calories 161, Calories from Fat 90, Total Fat 10g 15%, Protein 6.6g 13%, Points Value: 7

LUNCH

Mediterranean Veggie Wrap with Cilantro Hummus

Prep/Cook Time: 20 m , 4 servings

Ingredients

- Cilantro Hummus
- 1 clove garlic, peeled
- 1 (15 ounce) can no-salt-added garbanzo beans (chickpeas)
- 3 tablespoons lemon juice
- 2 tablespoons olive oil
- 1 tablespoon tahini (sesame seed paste)
- ¼ teaspoon sale
- ¼ teaspoon white pepper
- ¼ cup fresh cilantro leaves
- Mediterranean Wraps
- 4 cups mixed baby greens

- ½ large cucumber, halved lengthwise and sliced (1 cup)
- 1 cup chopped tomato
- ½ cup thinly sliced red onion
- ¼ cup crumbled reduced-fat feta cheese
- 2 tablespoons bottled sliced mild banana peppers
- 1 tablespoon balsamic vinegar
- 1 tablespoon olive oil
- 1 clove garlic, minced
- ¼ teaspoon black pepper
- 4 (8 inch) light tomato-flavored oval multi-grain wraps

Instructions

- To prepare Cilantro Hummus: With the motor running, drop 1 clove peeled garlic through the feed tube of a food processor fitted with a steel blade attachment; process until finely minced.
- Scrape down the sides of the bowl. Rinse and drain one 15-ounce can no-salt-added garbanzo beans (chickpeas).
- Add garbanzo beans, 3 tablespoons lemon juice, 2 tablespoons olive oil, 1 tablespoon tahini (sesame seed paste), ¼ teaspoon salt and ¼ teaspoon white pepper.
- Process until completely smooth, stopping to scrape down the sides as necessary. Add ¼ cup fresh cilantro leaves. Pulse several times or until cilantro is evenly distributed and chopped.
- Chill until ready to use (see Tip). To prepare Mediterranean Wraps: In a large bowl combine greens, cucumber, tomato, red onion, feta cheese and banana peppers. In a small bowl whisk together vinegar, olive oil, garlic and black pepper.
- Pour dressing mixture over greens mixture. Toss to combine.
- Spread each wrap with about 2½ tablespoons hummus. Top with dressed greens mixture.
- Roll up. Serve immediately.
- To make ahead: Hummus may be prepared and chilled up to 3 days before using.
- Serve with Mint-Berry Spritzer.

Nutritional info per serving : Serving size: 1 wrap and 2½ tablespoons hummus , 269 calories; 12 g fat(2 g sat); 13 g fiber; 35 g carbohydrates; 16 g protein; 15 mcg, Points Value: 17

DINNER

Mediterranean Artichoke and Red Pepper Roll-Ups

Prep/Total Time: 30 min, Makes 2 dozen

Ingredients

- 1 can (14 ounces) water-packed artichoke hearts, rinsed, drained and finely chopped
- 4 ounces cream cheese, softened
- 1/3 cup grated Parmesan cheese
- 1/4 cup crumbled feta cheese
- 2 green onions, thinly sliced
- 3 tablespoons prepared pesto
- 8 flour tortillas (8 inches), warmed
- 1 jar (7-1/2 ounces) roasted sweet red peppers, drained and cut into strips

SAUCE:

- 1 cup sour cream
- 1 tablespoon minced chives

Instructions

- In a small bowl, combine the artichokes, cream cheese, Parmesan cheese, feta cheese, green onions and pesto until blended. Spread 1/4 cup mixture over each tortilla; top with red peppers and roll up tightly.
- Place 1 in. apart on a greased baking sheet. Bake at 350° until heated through, 12-15 minutes. Cut into thirds. Meanwhile, in a small bowl, combine sour cream and chives. Serve with rolls.

Nutritional info per serving : 1 appetizer with 1 teaspoon sauce: 112 calories, 6g fat (3g saturated fat), 14mg cholesterol, 217mg sodium, 11g carbohydrate (1g sugars, 0 fiber), 4g protein. , Points Value: 3

Day 9

BREAKFAST

Greek Omelette Casserole

Prep Time 10 mins, Cook Time 35 mins , Servings: 12 pieces

Ingredients

- 12 large eggs
- 2 cups whole milk
- 8 ounces fresh spinach
- 2 cloves garlic, minced
- 12 ounces artichoke salad (with olives and peppers) drained and chopped
- 5 ounces sun dried tomato feta cheese, crumbled
- 1 tablespoon fresh chopped dill (1 teaspoon dried dill)
- 1 teaspoon dried oregano
- 1 teaspoon lemon pepper
- 1 teaspoon salt
- 4 teaspoons olive oil, divided

Instructions

- Preheat oven to 375 degrees F. Chop the fresh herbs and artichoke salad.
- Set a skillet over medium heat and add 1 tablespoon olive oil. Sauté the spinach and garlic until wilted, about 3 minutes.
- Oil a 9x13 inch baking dish and layer the spinach and artichoke salad evenly in the dish.
- In a medium bowl, whisk together the eggs, milk, herbs, salt and lemon pepper.
- Pour the egg mixture over vegetables and sprinkle with feta cheese. Bake in the center of the oven for 35-40 minutes until firm in the center.

Nutritional info per serving : Calories 186 Calories from Fat 117 , Total Fat 13g 20% , Saturated Fat 4g 20% , Cholesterol 225mg 75% , Protein 10g 20%, Points Value: 6

LUNCH

Tomato, Cucumber & White-Bean Salad with Basil Vinaigrette

Prep/Cook Time: 25 m, 4 servings

Ingredients

- ½ cup packed fresh basil leaves
- ¼ cup extra-virgin olive oil
- 3 tablespoons red-wine vinegar
- 1 tablespoon finely chopped shallot
- 2 teaspoons Dijon mustard
- 1 teaspoon honey
- ¼ teaspoon salt
- ¼ teaspoon ground pepper
- 10 cups mixed salad greens
- 1 (15 ounce) can low-sodium cannellini beans, rinsed
- 1 cup halved cherry or grape tomatoes
- ½ cucumber, halved lengthwise and sliced (1 cup)

Instructions

- Place basil, oil, vinegar, shallot, mustard, honey, salt and pepper in a mini food processor.
- Process until mostly smooth. Transfer to a large bowl.
- Add greens, beans, tomatoes and cucumber. Toss to coat.

Nutritional info per serving : 246 calories; 15 g fat(2 g sat); 8 g fiber; 22 g carbohydrates; 8 g protein; 190 mcg, Points Value: 13

DINNER

Walnut-Rosemary Crusted Salmon

Prep: 10 m, Cook time: 20 m, 4 servings

Ingredients

- 2 teaspoons Dijon mustard
- 1 clove garlic, minced
- ¼ teaspoon lemon zest
- 1 teaspoon lemon juice
- 1 teaspoon chopped fresh rosemary
- ½ teaspoon honey
- ½ teaspoon kosher salt
- ¼ teaspoon crushed red pepper
- 3 tablespoons panko breadcrumbs

- 3 tablespoons finely chopped walnuts
- 1 teaspoon extra-virgin olive oil
- 1 (1 pound) skinless salmon fillet, fresh or frozen
- Olive oil cooking spray

Instructions

- Preheat oven to 425°F. Line a large rimmed baking sheet with parchment paper.
- Combine mustard, garlic, lemon zest, lemon juice, rosemary, honey, salt and crushed red pepper in a small bowl. Combine panko, walnuts and oil in another small bowl.
- Place salmon on the prepared baking sheet. Spread the mustard mixture over the fish and sprinkle with the panko mixture, pressing to adhere. Lightly coat with cooking spray.
- Bake until the fish flakes easily with a fork, about 8 to 12 minutes, depending on thickness.

Nutritional info per serving : Serving size: 3 ounces , Per serving: 222 calories; 12 g fat(2 g sat); 0 g fiber; 4 g carbohydrates; 24 g protein; 62 mg, Points Value: 7

Day 10

BREAKFAST

Greek Guacamole

Prep/Done Time 10 minutes, Servings: (1/4-cup servings)

Ingredients

- 2 large ripe avocados (halved, pit removed)
- 2 Tbsp lemon juice
- 1 heaping Tbsp chopped sun-dried tomatoes
- 3 Tbsp diced ripe cherry tomato
- 1/4 cup diced red onion
- 1 tsp dried oregano (or sub fresh)
- 2 Tbsp fresh chopped parsley
- 4 whole kalamata olives (pitted and chopped // optional)
- 1 pinch each sea salt and black pepper

Instructions

- Add avocado and lemon juice to a large mixing bowl and use a potato masher, pastry cutter, or large fork to mash and mix.
- Add remaining ingredients (olives are optional), and stir to combine (see photo). Sample and add salt and pepper if needed.
- Adjust other flavors if needed, adding more lemon for acidity, sun-dried tomato for deeper tomato flavor, onion for crunch/spice, or parsley or oregano.
- Enjoy immediately with pita, pita chips, or vegetables! Best when fresh, though leftovers keep in the refrigerator for 2-3 days.

Nutritional info per serving : Calories: 110 Fat: 10g , Saturated fat: 2.1g , Sodium: 54mg , Carbohydrates: 5.7g , Protein: 1.2g, , Points Value: 4

LUNCH

Charcuterie Bistro Lunch Box

Prep+Cook Time: 5 m, 1 serving

Ingredients

- 1 slice prosciutto
- 1 mozzarella stick, halved
- 2 breadsticks, halved
- 2 dates
- ½ cup grapes
- Red Seedless Grapes 1 Lb
- 2 large radishes, halved or 4 slices English cucumber (¼-inch)

Instructions

- Cut prosciutto in half lengthwise, then wrap a slice around each portion of cheese.
- Arrange the wrapped cheese, breadsticks, dates, grapes and radishes (or cucumber) in a 4-cup divided sealable container.
- Keep refrigerated until ready to eat.
- To make ahead: Refrigerate for up to 1 day.

Nutritional info per serving : 452 calories; 18 g fat(6 g sat); 4 g fiber; 65 g carbohydrates; 17 g protein; 19 mcg, Points Value: 25

DINNER

Caprese Stuffed Portobello Mushrooms

Prep: 25 m, Cook time: 40 m, 4 servings

Ingredients

- 3 tablespoons extra-virgin olive oil, divided
- 1 medium clove garlic, minced
- ½ teaspoon salt, divided
- ½ teaspoon ground pepper, divided
- 4 portobello mushrooms (about 14 ounces), stems and gills removed (see Tip)
- 1 cup halved cherry tomatoes
- ½ cup fresh mozzarella pearls, drained and patted dry

- ½ cup thinly sliced fresh basil
- 2 teaspoons best-quality balsamic vinegar

Instructions

- Preheat oven to 400°F. Combine 2 tablespoons oil, garlic, ¼ teaspoon salt and ¼ teaspoon pepper in a small bowl. Using a silicone brush, coat mushrooms all over with the oil mixture.
- Place on a large rimmed baking sheet and bake until the mushrooms are mostly soft, about 10 minutes.
- Meanwhile, stir tomatoes, mozzarella, basil and the remaining ¼ teaspoon salt, ¼ teaspoon pepper and 1 tablespoon oil together in a medium bowl.
- Once the mushrooms have softened, remove from the oven and fill with the tomato mixture. Bake until the cheese is fully melted and the tomatoes have wilted, about 12 to 15 minutes more.
- Drizzle each mushroom with ½ teaspoon vinegar and serve.

Tip: To prepare portobello mushroom caps, gently twist off the stems of whole portobellos. Using a spoon, scrape off the brown gills from the underside of the mushroom caps. If you prefer, purchase portobello mushroom caps, rather than whole mushrooms.

Nutritional info per serving : Serving size: 1 mushroom , Per serving: 186 calories; 16 g fat(4 g sat); 2 g fiber; 6 g carbohydrates; 6 g protein; 37 mcg, Points Value: 6

Day 11

BREAKFAST

Gingerbread Breakfast Quinoa Bake with Banana

Prep Time 10 mins, Cook Time 1 hour 20 mins, Servings 8

Ingredients

- 3 cups Medium over-ripe ONE Bananas mashed (just under 1 1/2 or 370g)
- 1/4 Cup Molasses
- 1/4 Cup Pure maple syrup
- 1 Tbsp Cinnamon
- 2 tsps Raw vanilla extract
- 1 tsp Ground ginger
- 1 tsp Ground cloves
- 1/2 tsp Ground allspice
- 1/2 tsp Salt
- 1 Cup Quinoa uncooked
- 2 1/2 Cups Unsweetened vanilla almond milk
- 1/4 Cup Slivered almonds

Instructions

- In the bottom of a 2 1/2-3 quart casserole dish, stir together the mashed banana, molasses, maple syrup, cinnamon, vanilla extract, ginger, cloves, allspice and salt until well mixed. Add in the quinoa and stir until the quinoa is evenly distributed in the banana mixture.
- Whisk in the almond milk until well combined. Cover and refrigerate overnight. *
- In the morning, heat your oven to 350 degrees and whisk the quinoa mixture to make sure it hasn't settled to the bottom.
- Cover the pan with tinfoil and bake until the liquid is absorbed, and the top of the quinoa is set, about 1 hour -to 1 hour and 15 mins.
- Turn your oven to high broil, uncover the pan, sprinkle with sliced almonds, and lightly press them into the quinoa. Broil until the almonds just turn golden brown, about 2-4 minutes. Watch closely, as they burn quickly!
- Let cool for 10 minutes (it's HOT!) and DEVOUR.

Nutritional info per serving :Calories 213 , Calories from Fat 37 , Total Fat 4.1g 6% , Cholesterol 0mg 0%, Points Value: 8

LUNCH

Salmon and Couscous Casserole

Prep+Cook Time: 15 m, Cook time 25 mins, Servings : 4

Ingredients

- 1 cup water
- 2 cloves garlic, minced
- ⅔ cup whole wheat couscous
- 1 (14.75 ounce) can salmon, drained, flaked, and skin and bones removed
- 2 cups packaged fresh baby spinach leaves
- ½ cup jarred roasted red sweet peppers, drained and chopped
- ⅓ cup jarred tomato bruschetta topper
- 2 tablespoons purchased toasted almonds

Instructions

- In a 2-quart microwave-safe casserole, combine the water and garlic. Microwave, uncovered, on 100% power (high) for 2-½ to 3 minutes or until mixture is boiling. Remove from microwave and stir in couscous; spoon salmon atop couscous mixture. Cover and let stand for 5 minutes. Add spinach, roasted peppers, and bruschetta topper to couscous mixture. Toss to combine. Divide mixture among four serving plates. Top with almonds. Makes 4 servings (1-¼ cups each).
- Tip: If you cannot find toasted almonds, you can use untoasted almonds or toast your own. To toast your own, preheat oven to 350°F. Spread whole almonds in a single layer in a pie pan. Bake for 8 to 10 minutes or until lightly browned, stirring occasionally. Cool completely before using.

Nutritional info per serving : Serving size: 1¼ cups , 35 calories; 9 g fat(2 g sat); 6 g fiber; 34 g carbohydrates; 30 g protein; 51 mcg, Points Value: 3

DINNER

Greek Chicken with Roasted Spring Vegetables & Lemon Vinaigrette

Prep: 30 m, Cook: 50 m, 4 servings

Ingredients

- Lemon Vinaigrette
- 1 lemon

- 1 tablespoon olive oil
- 1 tablespoon crumbled feta cheese
- ½ teaspoon honey
- Greek Chicken with Roasted Spring Vegetables
- 2 (8 ounce) skinless, boneless chicken breast halves, cut in half lengthwise
- ¼ cup light mayonnaise
- 6 cloves garlic, minced
- ½ cup panko bread crumbs
- 3 tablespoons grated Parmesan cheese
- ½ teaspoon kosher salt
- ½ teaspoon black pepper
- Nonstick olive oil cooking spray
- 2 cups 1-inch pieces asparagus
- 1½ cups sliced fresh cremini mushrooms
- 1½ cups halved grape tomatoes
- 1 tablespoon olive oil
- Snipped fresh dill

Instructions

- Prepare vinaigrette: Remove ½ teaspoon zest and squeeze 1 tablespoon juice from lemon. In a small bowl whisk together lemon zest and juice and the remaining ingredients. Set aside. Prepare chicken and vegetables: Place a 15x10-inch baking pan in oven. Preheat oven to 475°F. Meanwhile, using the flat side of a meat mallet, flatten chicken between two pieces of plastic wrap until ½ inch thick. Place chicken in a medium bowl.
- Add mayonnaise and 2 of the garlic cloves; stir to coat. In a shallow dish stir together bread crumbs, cheese, ¼ teaspoon of the salt, and ¼ teaspoon of the pepper. Dip chicken into crumb mixture, turning to coat. Lightly coat tops of chicken with cooking spray.
- In a large bowl combine asparagus, mushrooms, tomatoes, oil and the remaining 4 cloves garlic and ¼ teaspoon salt and pepper.
- Carefully place chicken in one end of hot pan and place asparagus mixture in other end of pan. Roast 18 to 20 minutes or until chicken is done (165°F) and vegetables are tender.
- Drizzle chicken and vegetables with vinaigrette and sprinkle with dill.

Nutritional info per serving : Serving size: 3½ ounces chicken and ½ cup vegetables , Per serving: 306 calories; 15 g fat(3 g sat); 2 g fiber; 12 g carbohydrates; 29 g protein; 38 mcg, Points Value: 14

Day 12

BREAKFAST

Stuffed Sweet Potatoes with Chickpeas & Avocado Tahini

Prep Time 10 mins, Cook Time 40 mins, Servings: 8

Ingredients

- 8 medium sized sweet potatoes rinsed well

Marinated Chickpeas

- 1 15 oz can chickpeas drained and rinsed
- 1/2 red pepper diced
- 3 tablespoons extra virgin olive oil
- 1 tablespoon fresh lemon juice
- 1 tablespoon lemon zest
- 1 clove | about 1/2 teaspoon garlic crushed
- 1 tablespoon freshly chopped parsley
- 1 tablespoon fresh oregano
- 1/4 teaspoon sea salt

Avocado Tahini Sauce

- 1 medium sized ripe avocado
- 1/4 cup tahini
- 1/4 cup water
- 1 clove garlic crushed
- 1 tablespoons fresh parsley
- 1 tablespoon fresh lemon juice

Toppings

- 1/4 cup pepitas hulled pumpkin seeds
- crumbled up vegan feta or regular feta* to keep it dairy free

Instructions

- Preheat the oven to 400°F/ 204°C.
- Use a fork to pierce a few holes in your sweet potatoes to allow air to escape. Place them on a baking sheet and bake for 45 minutes to an hour or until tender to the touch. The large your sweet potato the longer they will need to bake.
- While the sweet potatoes are in the oven begin working on the chickpeas. In a medium sized bowl combine the chickpeas and the remaining ingredients needed for marinating. Toss the chickpeas until they're all coated in the marinade then set aside for later.

Avocado Tahini Sauce

- To make the sauce, add all of the sauce ingredients to a blender and process until smooth. If you want a thinned consistency add another 1-2 tablespoons of water. Once smooth transfer the sauce to a small bowl and set aside until needed.

Assembly

- Once the sweet potatoes are tender to the touch remove them from the oven and set aside until cool enough to handle. When you're ready cut a slit down the middle of each potato and carefully spoon the chickpeas inside. Top with the avocado tahini and sprinkle the pepitas over the top along with the crumpled up feta. These are best served fresh, but you can keep them in the fridge for up to 2 days

Nutritional info per serving : Calories 308 , Calories from Fat 135 , Total Fat 15g 23% , Protein 7g 14, Points Value: 13

LUNCH

Egg and Tomato Skillet with Pita (Shakshouka)

Prep +Cook time: 40 m, 4 servings

Ingredients

- 2 tablespoons olive oil
- 2 cups chopped red sweet peppers
- ½ cup chopped onion
- 2 tablespoons no-salt-added tomato paste
- 1 teaspoon smoked paprika
- 2 teaspoons crushed red pepper
- 3 cups chopped tomatoes
- 1 teaspoon ground cumin
- ¼ teaspoon salt
- 4 eggs
- ½ cup plain low-fat Greek yogurt
- Snipped fresh parsley
- 2 whole-wheat pita bread rounds, halved crosswise and warmed

Instructions

- In a 10-inch skillet heat oil over medium. Add the next five ingredients (through crushed red pepper). Cook 5 to 7 minutes or until onion is tender, stirring occasionally.
- Stir in tomatoes, cumin and salt. Bring to boiling; reduce heat. Simmer 10 minutes or until tomatoes begin to break down.

- Make four indentations in tomato mixture. Break an egg into a custard cup or small bowl and slip into an indentation.
- Repeat with remaining three eggs. Simmer, covered, 4 to 6 minutes or until whites are completely set and yolks begin to thicken but are not hard.
- Top with yogurt and sprinkle with parsley. Serve with pita bread.

Nutritional info per serving : Serving size: 1 cup , 303 calories; 13 g fat(3 g sat); 6 g fiber; 33 g carbohydrates; 15 g protein; 189 mg, Points Value: 16

DINNER

Mediterranean Bulgur Bowl

Prep/Total Time: 30 min, 4 servings

Ingredients

- 1 cup bulgur
- 1/2 teaspoon ground cumin
- 1/4 teaspoon salt
- 2 cups water
- 1 can (15 ounces) chickpeas or garbanzo beans, rinsed and drained
- 6 ounces fresh baby spinach (about 8 cups)
- 2 cups cherry tomatoes, halved
- 1 small red onion, halved and thinly sliced
- 1/2 cup crumbled feta cheese
- 1/4 cup hummus
- 2 tablespoons chopped fresh mint
- 2 tablespoons lemon juice

Instructions

- In a 6-qt. stockpot, combine first four ingredients; bring to a boil. Reduce heat; simmer, covered, until tender, 10-12 minutes. Stir in garbanzo beans; heat through.
- Remove from heat; stir in spinach. Let stand, covered, until spinach is wilted, about 5 minutes. Stir in remaining ingredients. Serve warm or refrigerate and serve cold.

Health Tip: With the spinach, tomatoes and feta cheese, this dish supplies all the vitamin A you need in a day.

Nutritional info per serving : 2 cups: 311 calories, 7g fat (2g saturated fat), 8mg cholesterol, 521mg sodium, 52g carbohydrate (6g sugars, 12g fiber), 14g protein. , Points Value: 16

Day 13

BREAKFAST

Mediterranean Tuna Salad

Prep Time 8 minutes, Servings 2

Ingredients

- 1 in can Wild Selections solid white albacore tuna water drained
- 2 Tablespoons capers
- 8 kalamata olives sliced
- 1/4 cup diced roasted red peppers
- 1 Tablespoon lemon juice
- 2 Tablespoons olive oil
- 1 Tablespoon chopped fresh flat-leaf parsley optional
- salt* and pepper to taste *I did not need any salt since the olives and capers had enough them to flavor the whole dish

Instructions

- Add all ingredients to a mixing bowl, and use a fork to flake apart the tuna and mix together.
- Serve immediately, or refrigerate leftovers.

Nutritional info per serving : Calories: 250kal , , Points Value: 8

LUNCH

Tomato Salad with Grilled Halloumi and Herbs

Prep: 8 min, Cook: 2 min, 4 servings

Ingredients

- 1 pound tomatoes, sliced into rounds
- ½ lemon
- Flaky salt and freshly ground pepper
- Extra-virgin olive oil
- ½ pound halloumi cheese, sliced into 4 slabs
- 5 basil leaves, torn
- 2 tablespoons finely chopped flat-leaf parsley

Instructions

- Preheat a grill or grill pan over medium-high heat.
- Arrange the tomatoes on a serving platter or four plates. Lightly squeeze the lemon over them and season with flaky salt and pepper.
- Brush the grill grates with oil, then add the halloumi and cook, turning once, until marks appear and the cheese is warmed throughout, about 1 minute per side. Place on top of the tomatoes. Drizzle the salad with olive oil and sprinkle with the basil and parsley. Serve immediately.

Nutritional info per serving : 196 calories , 15g fat , 8g carbs , 9g protein , 6g sugars , Points Value: 10

DINNER

Chicken with Tomato-Balsamic Pan Sauce

Prep: 35 m, Cook: 35 m, 4 servings

Ingredients

- 2 8-ounce boneless, skinless chicken breasts
- ½ teaspoon salt, divided
- ½ teaspoon ground pepper, divided
- ¼ cup white whole-wheat flour
- 3 tablespoons extra-virgin olive oil, divided
- ½ cup halved cherry tomatoes
- 2 tablespoons sliced shallot
- ¼ cup balsamic vinegar
- 1 cup low-sodium chicken broth
- 1 tablespoon minced garlic
- 1 tablespoon fennel seeds, toasted and lightly crushed
- 1 tablespoon butter

Instructions

- Remove and reserve chicken tenders (if attached) for another use. Slice each breast in half horizontally to make 4 pieces total. Place on a cutting board and cover with a large piece of plastic wrap.
- Pound with the smooth side of a meat mallet or a heavy saucepan to an even thickness of about ¼ inch. Sprinkle with ¼ teaspoon each salt and pepper. Place flour in a shallow dish and dredge the cutlets to coat both sides, shaking off excess. (Discard remaining flour.) Heat 2 tablespoons oil in a large skillet over medium-high heat.

- Add 2 pieces of chicken and cook, turning once, until evenly browned and cooked through, 2 to 3 minutes per side. Transfer to a large serving plate and tent with foil to keep warm. Repeat with the remaining chicken. Add the remaining 1 tablespoon oil, tomatoes and shallot to the pan. Cook, stirring occasionally, until softened, 1 to 2 minutes.
- Add vinegar; bring to a boil. Cook, scraping up any browned bits from the bottom of the pan, until the vinegar is reduced by about half, about 45 seconds.
- Add broth, garlic, fennel seeds and the remaining ¼ teaspoon salt and pepper. Cook, stirring, until the sauce is reduced by about half, 4 to 7 minutes. Remove from heat; stir in butter. Serve the sauce over the chicken.

Nutritional info per serving : Per serving: 294 calories; 17 g fat(4 g sat); 1 g fiber; 9 g carbohydrates; 25 g protein; 8 mcg, Points Value: 12

Day 14

BREAKFAST

Greek Salad Sushi

Prep/Done Time 10 minutes, Servings 10 rolls

Ingredients

- 1 cucumber
- 1/2 cup plain Greek yogurt 120 g
- 2 tsp lemon juice 10 mL
- 1 clove garlic minced
- 1 tsp fresh dill chopped
- Salt and pepper to taste
- 1/2 bell pepper finely diced
- 1/4 cup finely diced red onion 30 g
- 1/4 cup crumbled feta cheese 30 g

Instructions

- Peel: Chop the ends off of the cucumber and use a mandolin or vegetable peeler to peel thin slices along, lengthwise. Set slices on a few layers of paper towels and cover with a few more. Pat to dry and let sit while you make the tzatziki.
- Tzatziki: To make tzatziki, combine, yogurt, lemon, garlic, dill, salt, and pepper.
- Roll: Spread some tzatziki onto a cucumber slice. Top with pepper, onion, and feta. Roll up and secure with a toothpick. Continue until you have used all your ingredients.

Nutritional info per serving : Calories 54 , Calories from Fat 20 , Total Fat 2.2g 3% , Cholesterol 9mg 3%, Points Value: 2

LUNCH

Harissa Chickpea Stew with Eggplant and Millet

Prep: 35 min, Cook: 10 min, 2 servings

Ingredients

- 1 cup millet
- Kosher salt
- 2 tablespoons ghee (or another neutral high-heat oil), divided
- 1 large Japanese eggplant
- Freshly ground black pepper
- 1 onion, diced
- 3 garlic cloves, minced
- One fourteen-ounce can pureed tomatoes
- One fourteen-ounce can chickpeas, drained
- 2 tablespoons harissa paste
- 1 bunch cilantro, for garnish

Instructions

- Fill a medium saucepan with 2 cups water and add the millet and a pinch of salt. Bring to a boil, cover, reduce to a simmer and cook for 25 minutes. Once the millet is done cooking, remove the lid, fluff with a fork and allow to cool.
- Meanwhile, heat 1 tablespoon of ghee or oil in a deep skillet over medium heat. Add the eggplant, season with salt and pepper, and cook until tender and golden brown, adding more ghee as necessary to prevent the eggplant from sticking to the skillet, about 10 minutes. Transfer the eggplant to a bowl and set it aside.
- Add the remaining 1 tablespoon of ghee or oil to the same skillet, add the onion and cook until soft and golden brown, 8 to 10 minutes.
- Add the garlic and cook for 2 more minutes. Season with salt and pepper, and then add the tomatoes, chickpeas and harissa. Return the eggplant to the skillet and reduce the heat to low; allow to simmer for 10 to 15 minutes.
- Divide the millet between two bowls and top with the stew. Garnish with a few leaves of cilantro and serve warm.

Nutritional info per serving : 600 calories , 15g fat , 100g carbs , 20g protein , 17g sugars , Points Value: 22

DINNER

Chicken Souvlaki Kebabs with Mediterranean Couscous

Prep: 45 m, Cook: 2 h 20 m, Servings : 4

Ingredients

- Chicken Souvlaki Kabobs
- 1 pound skinless, boneless chicken breast halves, cut into ½-inch strips
- 1 cup sliced fennel (reserve leaves, if desired)
- ⅓ cup dry white wine
- ¼ cup lemon juice
- 3 tablespoons canola oil
- 4 cloves garlic, minced
- 2 teaspoons dried oregano, crushed
- ½ teaspoon salt
- ¼ teaspoon black pepper
- Lemon wedges
- Mediterranean Couscous
- 1 teaspoon olive oil
- ½ cup Israeli (large pearl) couscous
- 1 cup water
- ½ cup snipped dried tomatoes (not oil-packed)
- ¾ cup chopped red sweet pepper
- ½ cup chopped cucumber
- ½ cup chopped red onion
- ⅓ cup plain fat-free Greek yogurt
- ¼ cup thinly sliced fresh basil leaves
- ¼ cup snipped fresh parsley
- 1 tablespoon lemon juice
- ¼ teaspoon salt
- ¼ teaspoon black pepper

Instructions

- Prepare kabobs: Place chicken and sliced fennel in a resealable plastic bag set in a shallow dish. For marinade, in a small bowl combine the white wine, lemon juice, oil, garlic, oregano, salt and pepper. Remove ¼ cup of the marinade and set aside.
- Pour the remaining marinade over chicken mixture. Seal bag; turn to coat chicken mixture. Marinate in the refrigerator 1½ hours, turning bag once. Meanwhile, if using wooden skewers, soak eight 10- to 12-inch skewers in water 30 minutes.
- Drain chicken, discarding marinade and fennel. Thread chicken, accordion-style, onto skewers. Grill chicken skewers, covered, over medium-high heat 6 to 8 minutes or until chicken is no longer pink,

- turning once. Remove from grill and brush with the reserved ¼ cup marinade.
- Prepare couscous: In a small saucepan heat 1 teaspoon olive oil over medium heat. Add ½ cup Israeli (large pearl) couscous. Cook and stir 4 minutes or until light brown. Add 1 cup water.
- Bring to boiling; reduce heat. Simmer, covered, 10 minutes or until couscous is tender and liquid is absorbed, adding ½ cup snipped dried tomatoes (not oil-packed) the last 5 minutes; cool.
- Transfer couscous to a large bowl. Stir in ¾ cup chopped red sweet pepper, ½ cup each chopped cucumber and chopped red onion, ⅓ cup plain fat-free Greek yogurt, ¼ cup each thinly sliced fresh basil leaves and snipped fresh parsley, 1 tablespoon lemon juice and ¼ teaspoon each salt and black pepper.
- Serve kabobs with couscous, lemon wedges and, if desired, reserved fennel leaves.

Nutritional info per serving : 332 calories; 9 g fat(1 g sat); 2 g fiber; 28 g carbohydrates; 32 g protein; 46 mcg, Points Value: 17

Day 15

BREAKFAST

Zucchini and Tomato Frittata

Prep/Cook Time: 30 minutes, 4 Servings

Ingredients:

- 2 tsp olive oil
- 1 medium onion, diced
- 1-1/2 cups (7 oz) zucchini, diced into matchsticks
- 4 large eggs
- 4 large egg whites
- 1/4 cup Asiago cheese, grated
- salt and fresh pepper
- 2 medium (about 8 oz) vine ripe tomatoes, cored and thinly sliced crosswise

Instructions

- Preheat oven to 400°F.
- Heat oil in a 10-inch skillet over medium-low heat. Stir in onion and cook until slightly golden, about 8 to 10 minutes. Add zucchini, increase heat to medium-high, season with salt and pepper and cook 2 to 3 minutes or until the moisture dries up, stirring occasionally.
- In a medium bowl whisk eggs, egg whites, Asiago, salt and pepper.
- Pour the eggs into the skillet making sure they cover all the vegetables. Arrange tomatoes in an overlapping pattern on top and season with salt and pepper. When the edges begin to set (about 2 minutes) move skillet to oven. Cook about 16 to 18 minutes, or until frittata is completely cooked. Serve warm, cut into 4 pieces.

Nutritional info per serving : Calories: 172 calories , Total Fat: 10g , Saturated Fat: g , Protein: 13g, Points Value: 4

LUNCH

Grilled Lemon-Herb Chicken and Avocado Salad

Prep: 35 min, Cook: 1 hr, 4 servings

Ingredients

Lemon-Herb Chicken

- 1½ pounds boneless, skinless chicken breasts
- 3 tablespoons extra-virgin olive oil
- Zest and juice of 2 lemons
- 1 tablespoon chopped fresh oregano
- 1 tablespoon chopped fresh dill
- 3 tablespoons chopped fresh parsley
- Kosher salt and freshly ground black pepper

Salad

- 1 cup barley
- 2½ cups chicken broth
- Zest and juice of 1 lemon
- 1 tablespoon whole-grain mustard
- 1 teaspoon dried oregano
- ⅓ cup extra-virgin olive oil
- Kosher salt and freshly ground black pepper
- 2 heads red-leaf lettuce, chopped
- 1 red onion, halved and thinly sliced
- 1 pint cherry tomatoes, sliced
- 2 avocados, sliced

Instructions

- MAKE THE LEMON-HERB CHICKEN: Place the chicken in a large resealable plastic bag. In a medium bowl, whisk together the olive oil, lemon zest, lemon juice, oregano, dill and parsley. Pour the marinade into the bag, seal it and refrigerate for 30 minutes.
- MAKE THE SALAD: Meanwhile, in a medium saucepan, bring the barley and chicken broth to a simmer over medium heat. When it comes to a simmer, cover the pot and cook until the barley is tender, 35 to 45 minutes. Drain and reserve.
- In a medium bowl, whisk together the lemon zest, lemon juice, mustard and oregano. Gradually stream in the olive oil and whisk well to combine. Season with salt and pepper.
- Prepare your grill for high heat. Remove the chicken from the marinade and season with salt and pepper.
- Grill the chicken until well charred on both sides and fully cooked through, flipping as needed, 10 to 12 minutes. Remove the chicken from the grill and reserve.

- In a large bowl, toss together the lettuce, onion and tomatoes. Add the dressing and toss well to coat.
- Slice the chicken and serve on top of the salad alongside the avocado.

Nutritional info per serving : 309 calories , 15g fat , 4g carbs , 39g protein , 1g sugars , Salad : 602 calories, Points Value: 10

DINNER

Hasselback Caprese Chicken

Prep 25 m Cook: 50 m, 4 servings

Ingredients

- 2 boneless, skinless chicken breasts (8 ounces each)
- ½ teaspoon salt, divided
- ½ teaspoon ground pepper, divided
- 1 medium tomato, sliced
- 3 ounces fresh mozzarella, halved and sliced
- ¼ cup prepared pesto
- 8 cups broccoli florets
- 2 tablespoons extra-virgin olive oil

Instructions

- Preheat oven to 375°F. Coat a large rimmed baking sheet with cooking spray.
- Make crosswise cuts every ½ inch along both chicken breasts, slicing almost to the bottom but not all the way through. Sprinkle chicken with ¼ teaspoon each salt and pepper.
- Fill the cuts alternately with tomato and mozzarella slices. Brush with pesto.
- Transfer the chicken to one side of the prepared baking sheet. Toss broccoli, oil and the remaining ¼ teaspoon each salt and pepper in a large bowl.
- If there are any tomato slices left, mix them in. Transfer the broccoli mixture to the empty side of the baking sheet.
- Bake until the chicken is no longer pink in the center and the broccoli is tender, about 25 minutes.
- Cut each breast in half and serve with the broccoli.

Nutrition Info : Serving size: ½ chicken breast & 1 cup vegetables , 355 calories; 19 g fat(6 g sat); 4 g fiber; 10 g carbohydrates; 38 g protein; 117 mcg, Points Value: 20

Day 16

BREAKFAST

Watermelon Feta and Balsamic "Pizzas"

Prep+ Cook Time: 15 minutes

Ingredients:

- 1 watermelon slice, cut 1-inch thick from center of the widest part
- 1 oz crumbled Feta cheese
- 5 to 6 Kalamata Olives, sliced
- 1 tsp mint leaves
- 1/2 tbsp balsamic glaze

Instructions

- Slice the widest part of a round watermelon in half. Lay the flat side down on a cutting board and cut a 1-inch thick slice from each half. Cut each half into 4 wedges.
- Place them on a round dish like a pizza and top with cheese, olives, balsamic glaze and mint leaves.

Nutritional info per serving : Calories: 90 calories , Total Fat: 3g, Points Value: 3

LUNCH

30 Minute Greek Shrimp and Farro Bowls

Prep time: 10 mins, Cook time: 20 mins, Serves: 4

Ingredients

- 1 lb. peeled and deveined shrimp
- 3 Tbsp. extra virgin olive oil
- 2 cloves garlic, minced
- Juice of 1 lemon
- 2 tsp. fresh chopped dill
- 1 Tbsp. fresh chopped oregano
- ½ tsp smoked paprika
- ½ tsp sea salt
- ¼ tsp black pepper
- 1 cup dry farro
- 2 bell peppers, sliced thick
- 2 medium-sized zucchinis, sliced into thin rounds
- 1 pint cherry tomatoes, halved

- ¼ cup thinly sliced green or black olives
- 4 Tbsp. 2% reduced-fat plain Greek yogurt

Instructions

- Place olive oil, garlic, lemon, dill, oregano, paprika, salt, and pepper in a bowl. Whisk to combine. Pour ~3/4 the amount of marinade over shrimp; toss to coat. Let stand 10 minutes.
- Cook farro according to package instructions in water or stock.
- Heat a grill pan or nonstick skillet over medium heat. Add shrimp; cook 2-3 minutes per side, until no longer pink; transfer to a plate.
- Add vegetables in batches to grill pan or skillet (avoid overcrowding); cook 5-6 minutes, until softened. Repeat with remaining vegetables.
- Divide cooked farro evenly among 4 bowls. Top evenly with shrimp, grilled vegetables, olives, and tomatoes. Drizzle reserved marinade overtop. Top each bowl with 1 Tbsp. Greek yogurt and extra lemon juice, if desired.

Nutritional info per serving : Serving size: 1 bowl Calories: 428 Fat: 13.5 gm Saturated fat: 2 gm Carbohydrates: 45 gm Sugar: 6 gm Sodium: 540 mg Fiber: 6 gm Protein: 34 gm Cholesterol: 174 mg, Points Value: 19

DINNER

Simple Grilled Salmon & Vegetables

Prep: 25 m, Cook time 25 m, 4 servings

Ingredients

- 1 medium zucchini, halved lengthwise
- 2 red, orange and/or yellow bell peppers, trimmed, halved and seeded
- 1 medium red onion, cut into 1-inch wedges
- 1 tablespoon extra-virgin olive oil
- ½ teaspoon salt, divided
- ½ teaspoon ground pepper
- 1¼ pounds salmon fillet, cut into 4 portions
- ¼ cup thinly sliced fresh basil
- 1 lemon, cut into 4 wedges

Instructions

- Preheat grill to medium-high. Brush zucchini, peppers and onion with oil and sprinkle with ¼ teaspoon salt. Sprinkle salmon with pepper and the remaining ¼ teaspoon salt.
- Place the vegetables and the salmon pieces, skin-side down, on the grill.
- Cook the vegetables, turning once or twice, until just tender and grill marks appear, 4 to 6 minutes per side.
- Cook the salmon, without turning, until it flakes when tested with a fork, 8 to 10 minutes. When cool enough to handle, roughly chop the vegetables and toss together in a large bowl.
- Remove the skin from the salmon fillets (if desired) and serve alongside the vegetables. Garnish each serving with 1 tablespoon basil and serve with a lemon wedge.

Nutritional info per serving : Serving size: 1¼ cups vegetables & 1 piece salmon , 281 calories; 13 g fat(2 g sat) , Points Value: 9

Day 17

BREAKFAST

Mediterranean scrambled eggs

Prep Time 5 mins, Cook Time 10 mins, Servings: 2

Ingredients

- 1 tbsp oil
- 1 yellow pepper, diced
- 2 spring onions, sliced
- 8 cherry tomatoes, quartered
- 2 tbsp sliced black olives
- 1 tbsp capers
- 4 eggs
- 1/4 tsp dried oregano
- Black pepper
- Fresh parsley, to serve (optional)

Instructions

- Heat the oil in a frying pan, and add the diced pepper and chopped spring onions. Cook for a few minutes over a medium heat, until slightly soft. Add the quartered tomatoes, olives and capers, and cook for 1 more minute.
- Crack the eggs into the pan, and immediately scramble with a spoon or spatula. Add the oregano and plenty of black pepper, and keep stirring until the eggs are fully cooked. Serve warm, topped with fresh parsley if desired.

Nutritional info per serving : Calories 249 , Calories from Fat 153 , Total Fat 17g 26% , Saturated Fat 3.8g 20%, Points Value: 13

LUNCH

Greek Lemon Chicken Soup

Prep Time: 10 mins, Cook Time: 20 mins, Servings: 8 Servings

Ingredients

- 10 cups chicken broth
- 3 tablespoon olive oil
- 8 cloves garlic, minced
- 1 sweet onion
- 1 large lemon, zested
- 2 boneless skinless chicken breasts
- 1 cup israeli (pearl) couscous
- 1/2 teaspoons crushed red pepper
- 2 ounces crumbled feta
- 1/3 cup chopped chive
- Salt and pepper

Instructions

- Place the olive oil in a large 6-8 quart sauce pot over medium-low heat. Peel the onion. Then quarter it and slice into thin strips. Once the oil is hot, saute the onion and minced garlic for 3-4 minutes to soften.
- Add the chicken broth, raw chicken breasts, lemon zest, and crushed red pepper to the pot. Raise the heat to high, cover, and bring to a boil. Once boiling, reduce the heat to medium, then simmer for 5 minutes.
- Stir in the couscous, 1 teaspoon salt, and black pepper to taste. Simmer another 5 minutes. Then turn the heat off.
- Using tongs, remove the two chicken breasts from the pot. Use a fork and the tongs to shred the chicken. Then place it back in the pot. Stir in the crumbled feta cheese and chopped chive. Taste and salt and pepper as needed. Serve warm.

Nutritional info per serving : Calories 286 , Calories from Fat 99 , Total Fat 11g 17% , Total Carbohydrates 31g 10% ,Protein 15g 30%, Points Value: 13

DINNER

Grilled Avocado Stuffed with Chickpeas and Tahini

Prep Time 10 mins, Cook Time 25 mins, Servings 4

Ingredients

- 1 Can Chickpeas drained and rinsed, 13oz
- Pompeian Grapeseed Oil Spray
- 1/2 tsp Smoked paprika
- Salt + Pepper
- 2 Large avocados
- 1/2 Cup Cucumber diced (about half a large cucumber)
- 1/2 Cup Cherry tomatoes cut into quarters
- 1 1/2 Tbsp Fresh lemon juice + additional for servings about 1 large lemon
- 2 tsps Tahini
- Cilantro for garnish

Instructions

- Preheat your grill to medium/high heat. The temperature gauge should read about 400 degress once heated.
- Place the rinsed chickpeas onto a paper towel and dry well. Transfer to a small bowl, peeling off any of the papery skins that come lose while you dried the chickpeas. Spray the chickpeas generously with Pompeian Grapeseed Oil Spray and then toss with the smoked paprika and a a few generous twists of salt and pepper.
- Place the chickpeas into the bottom of the grill basketinto an even, flat layer. Place onto the grill and cook for 10 minutes. Then, spray the chickpeas again with Pompeian Grapeseed Oil Spray and stir around. Cook for another 10-12 minutes until lightly charred and crispy. Remove from heat and let cool.
- Cut the avocados in half, removing the pit. Scoop out the center of the avocado so you have a large, deep hole. Spray the avocados with Pompeian Grapeseed Oil Spray and sprinkle with salt and pepper. Place, flesh-side down, onto the grill and cool until nice grill-marks form, about 5 minutes.

- While the avocados cook, mix the cucumber, tomatoes and lemon juice in a small bowl. Season with a pinch of salt and pepper.
- Divide the cucumber mixture between each avocado half, making sure to really stuff it into the center. Top each half with 1 Tbsp of chickpeas* and drizzle with 1/2 tsp Tahini.
- Garnish with cilantro and DEVOUR.

Recipe Notes : You will not use all of the chickpeas in this recipe, only about 1/3 of the can. But, it's easier to just grill the whole can and then snack on the extra crispy chickpea goodness!

Nutritional info per serving : Calories 206 kcal, Points Value: 6

Day 18

BREAKFAST

Smoked Salmon + Poached Eggs on Toast

Prep Time 10 minutes, Cook Time 4 minutes, Serves : 2

Ingredients

- 2 slices of bread toasted
- 2 oz avocado smashed
- 1/4 tsp freshly squeezed lemon juice
- Pinch of kosher salt and cracked black pepper
- 3.5 oz smoked salmon
- 2 eggs see notes, poached
- Splash of Kikkoman soy sauce optional
- 1 TBSP thinly sliced scallions
- Microgreens optional

Instructions

- In a small bowl, smash the avocado. Add the lemon juice and a pinch of salt; mix well and set aside.
- Poach your eggs and, when they are sitting in the ice bath, toast your bread.
- Once your bread is toasted, spread the avocado on both slices and add the smoked salmon to each slice.
- Carefully transfer the poached eggs to their respective toasts.
- Hit with a splash of Kikkoman soy sauce and some cracked pepper; garnish with scallions and microgreens.

Nutritional info per serving : Calories: 388.4 , Total Fat: 17.2 g , Protein: 33.5 g , Saturated Fat: 4.1 g, Points Value: 14

LUNCH

Chicken & Spring Vegetable Tortellini Salad

Prep+Cook: 30 m, 6 servings

Ingredients

- 1 pound boneless, skinless chicken breast
- 2 bay leaves
- 6 cups water
- 1 (20 ounce) package fresh cheese tortellini
- ½ cup peas, fresh or frozen
- ¼ cup creamy salad dressing, such as ranch or peppercorn
- 2 tablespoons red-wine vinegar
- 5 tablespoons chopped fresh herbs, such as basil, dill and/or chives, divided
- ½ cup chopped marinated artichokes plus 2 tablespoons marinade, divided
- ½ cup julienned radishes
- 1 cup pea shoots or baby arugula
- 2 tablespoons sunflower seeds

Instructions

- Combine chicken, bay leaves and water in a large saucepan. Bring to a boil over high heat. Reduce heat to low, cover and simmer until an instant-read thermometer inserted in the thickest part registers 165°F, 10 to 12 minutes.
- Transfer the chicken to a clean cutting board to cool. Remove the bay leaves. Add tortellini to the pot and return the water to a boil; cook, stirring occasionally, until the tortellini are just tender, about 3 minutes.
- Add peas and cook 1 minute more. Drain and rinse with cold water. Meanwhile, combine dressing, vinegar, 3 tablespoons herbs and artichoke marinade in a large bowl.
- Shred the chicken and add to the dressing along with the tortellini, peas, artichokes, radishes and pea shoots (or arugula); stir to combine. Serve the salad topped with the remaining 2 tablespoons herbs and sunflower seeds.

Nutritional info per serving : Serving size: 1½ cups , 357 calories; 13 g fat(3 g sat); 4 g fiber; 36 g carbohydrates; 24 g protein; 20 mcg, Points Value: 18

DINNER

Sweet Potato Falafel + Pumpkin Seed Chimichurri Sauce

Prep + Cook: 25 mins, Servings: 16 falafel

Ingredients

- Sweet Potato Falafel:
- 1 1/4 cups mashed sweet potato (boiled or baked)
- 1/3 cup nutritional yeast
- 1 1/2 cups chickpeas (cooked)
- 1/3 cup ground pumpkin seeds, raw
- 1 Tbsp maple syrup
- 1/2 tsp salt
- 2 tsp warming spices (I used a mixture of smoked paprika, cumin, chili powder and turmeric)
- 1/2 cup flat leaf parsley, finely chopped

- 1/4 cup lemon juice
- 1/4 cup extra virgin olive oil
- 1 cup flat leaf parsley, tightly packed
- 1/4 cup pumpkin seeds, raw
- 2 cloves garlic
- 1/4 tsp red chili flakes
- 1/4 tsp lemon zest
- 1/4 tsp salt
- 1/4 - 1/2 cup water (depending on desired consistency + boldness of sauce)
- Additional: extra virgin olive oil for coating falafel (optional)

Chimichurri Sauce:

Instructions

- Preheat oven to 415 degrees. Line a baking sheet with non-stick liner or grease with olive oil.
- In a large mixing bowl, mash all the falafel ingredients together until well combined.
- Form the falafel mixture into balls and place on baking sheet. If desired, you can roll entire ball in oil -- or simply brush the tops with oil. Or you can omit oil completely.
- Bake falafel balls at 415 degrees for 20-25 minutes or until edges brown. Optional: for crispier falafel, finish the falafel balls by sauteeing in oil in a skillet, over high heat, on the stovetop.

- For the sauce: blend all the sauce ingredients in a blender or food processor until smooth and creamy. (Start off with 1/4 cup water and add more for a thinner consistency, mellower flavor).
- Serving suggestions: Use falafels to fill pita pockets, along with hummus, vegan mayo, chopped greens and the chimichurri sauce. Sriracha optional. Pickled veggies or sauerkraut would also be a nice addition. Or serve over top a salad or grain bowl. Store leftover falafel in the fridge and reheat in microwave, oven or in a skillet on the stove. Enjoy!

Nutritional info per serving : Calories: 50 , carbs: 10g , protein: 2.5g , fiber: 2g, Points Value: 1

Day 19

BREAKFAST

Honey Almond Ricotta Spread with Fruit

Total Time:15 minutes, Serves 4-6

Ingredients:

For the ricotta spread:

- 1 cup whole milk ricotta
- 1/2 cup Fisher Sliced Almonds
- 1/4 teaspoon almond extract
- 1 teaspoons honey
- zest from an orange, optional

For serving:

- hearty whole grain toast, english muffin or bagel
- sliced peaches
- extra Fisher sliced almonds
- extra honey for drizzling

Instructions:

- Combine ricotta, almonds and almond extract in a medium sized mixing bowl and gently stir to combine. Transfer to a serving bowl and sprinkle with additional sliced almonds and drizzle with a teaspoon of honey.
- To serve, toast your bread. Spread 1 tablespoon of ricotta spread on each piece of bread. Top with sliced peaches, sliced almonds and honey.

Nutritional info per serving : 187 cal , Points Value: 6

LUNCH

Gluten-Free Pasta Salad Mediterranean Style

Prep Time: 15 mins, Cook time: 40 mins, Serves 6-8

Ingredients:

- 1 pint cherry tomatoes
- 2 medium Chinese eggplants, diced into small cubes
- Avocado (or olive) oil
- 1 teaspoon salt
- Pinch black pepper
- 1/4 teaspoon ground cumin
- 1/4 teaspoon red pepper flakes
- 1/4 teaspoon granulated garlic
- 1 (16 ounce) package brown rice spaghetti, cooked according to package instructions and cooled
- Lemon Dressing (recipe below)
- 1 tablespoon finely chopped dill
- 1 tablespoon finely chopped mint
- 1 tablespoon finely chopped parsley
- 1 tablespoon finely chopped cilantro

Instructions:

- -Preheat the oven to 400°, and line a baking sheet with parchment paper.
- -In a large bowl, toss together the cherry tomatoes, diced eggplant, about 3-4 tablespoons of the oil, the salt, pepper, cumin, red pepper flakes and granulated garlic, and turn out onto the parchment-lined baking sheet to bake/roast for 30-35 minutes, until slightly golden and tender; then, allow to cool slightly.
- -Place the cooked and cooled brown rice pasta into a large bowl, pour in some of the lemon dressing (go slow until you get your desired amount), and add in the cooled cherry tomato/eggplant mixture; sprinkle in the chopped herbs and toss everything together gently, and taste to see if any additional salt/pepper or dressing is needed; serve immediately, or keep covered and chilled in the fridge to serve later.

Lemon Dressing Ingredients:

- 4 large cloves garlic (or 6 small), pressed through garlic press
- Zest of 1 lemon
- 1/4 cup lemon juice
- 1/4 teaspoon salt
- Pinch black pepper
- 1/2 teaspoon dijon mustard
- 1/4 teaspoon granulated sugar
- 1/2 cup olive oil

Instructions:

- -Place all ingredients into a medium-size mason jar, seal the top, and shake vigorously to emulsify; use immediately, or keep cool in the fridge. (Use any remaining dressing on other salads, avocado slices, etc.)

Nutritional info per serving : *284 calories*, Points Value: 9

DINNER

Grilled Chicken + Dill Greek Yogurt Sauce

Prep Time: 10 mins, Cook Time: 12 mins, Servings: 8

Ingredients

For the Dill Greek Yogurt Sauce:

- 1 garlic clove, minced
- 1 cup chopped fresh dill, stems removed
- 1 1/4 cup Greek yogurt
- 1 tbsp olive oil
- Juice of 1/2 lemon or lime
- Pinch cayenne pepper, optional
- Salt, if needed

For the Grilled Chicken:

- 10 garlic cloves, minced
- 1/2 tsp paprika
- 1/2 tsp allspice
- 1/2 tsp ground nutmeg
- 1/4 tsp ground green cardamom
- Salt and pepper
- 5 tbsp olive oil, divided
- 8 boneless, skinless chicken thighs
- 1 medium size red onion, sliced
- Juice of 1-2 lemons

Instructions

- First make the dill Greek yogurt sauce. Combine the minced garlic, fresh dill, yogurt, olive oil, lemon juice and cayenne pepper in a food processor. Run the food processor until all the ingredients are well

- blended and a smooth thick sauce or dip develops. Test and add salt if needed. Transfer to a small bowl or container, cover and refrigerate.
    - In a small bowl, mix together the minced garlic, spices and 3 tbsp olive oil. Pat the chicken thighs dry and rub each with the garlic-spice mixture.
    - Place the spiced chicken thighs in a large dish on a bed of sliced red onions with lemon juice and the remaining 2 tbsp olive oil. Cover and refrigerate for 2-4 hours or overnight.
    - When ready, heat a gas grill to medium-high. Place the chicken thighs on the grill. Cover for 5-6 minutes, then turn the chicken over and grill for another 5-6 minutes covered.
    - Serve with a side of the dill Greek yogurt dip you prepared earlier!
    - To complete this light meal, add Greek potatoes or pita bread and a salad like Fattoush Salad.

Nutritional info per serving : Calories 172 , Total Fat 12.8g 20% , Trans Fat 0g , Total Carbohydrate 11.2g 4% , Sugars 4g , Protein 6g 12%, Points Value: 8

Day 20

BREAKFAST

Mediterranean Egg Cups with Goat Cheese

Prep Time: 30 Min, Cook Time: 15, 6 servings

Ingredients

- olive oil or coconut oil cooking spray
- 10 eggs
- 2/3 cup plain almond milk
- 1/2 tsp garlic powder
- 1/8 tsp salt
- 1/4 tsp black pepper pepper
- 1 1/2 cups chopped mushrooms
- 1 1/2 cups chopped roasted bell peppers, rinsed, drained and excess liquid blotted with a clean towel or paper towel

Topping:

- fresh basil leaves, torn
- goat cheese crumbles (1 1/4 Tbs {1/4 Blue} - 2 1/2 Tbs {1/2 Blue} per serving - you decide!)

Instructions

- Preheat your oven to 350 degrees. Prepare a 12 cup muffin tin by spraying it with cooking spray, making sure you spray on top too in case they go over a bit! Set aside.
- In a large bowl, whisk together the eggs, almond milk, garlic powder (not salt!), salt and black pepper until fully combined. Stir in the mushrooms and roasted peppers, then fill each muffin cup with the mixture. You'll use ALL of the mixture and they'll be pretty full, that's ok! (I used an ice cream scoop for this, it took about 2 scoops per cup and worked really well).
- Bake for 25 minutes or until set.
- Remove from oven, let them cool in the pan for 5-10 minutes or so (they'll deflate a bit, that's normal) then remove from the muffin tin.
- Serve with some torn basil and the goat cheese crumbles. Enjoy!

Nutritional info per serving : Serving Size: 2 egg cups with goat cheese , Calories per serving: 168 , Fiber per serving: 11 grams, Points Value: 5

LUNCH

Falafel Kale Salad with The Best Tahini Dressing

Prep Time 10 mins, Cook Time 30 mins, Servings 4

Ingredients

- 4-6 cups kale cut in bite-sized pieces and stems removed
- 1-2 lemons juiced
- 1 recipe Simple Crispy Vegan Falafel 12 balls
- 1 recipe The Best Tahini Dressing
- 1/2 red onion thinly sliced
- 15 oz can white beans drained and rinsed
- 1 jalapeño finely chopped (optional)
- 2 slices pita bread cut in square

Instructions

- Place the kale in a large bowl and drizzle with lemon juice. You may need to use more than one lemon depending on how how juicy your lemons are. Massage your kale for 60 seconds - incorporating the lemon juice into the kale. Place in the fridge until ready to use.

- Prepare Tahini Dressing according to instructions and place in the fridge until ready to use.
- Prepare the Simple Crispy Vegan Falafel according to instructions.
- Assemble salads: Divide kale between four bowls. Top each bowl with 3 falafel balls, red onion, white beans, jalapeño (if using) and pita slices. Drizzle dressing over each bowl. Serve and enjoy.

Nutritional info per serving : Total Fat 39.1 g 60% , Saturated Fat 10.2 g 51% , Cholesterol 0% , Sodium 1139 mg 47%, Points Value: 13

DINNER

Easy Peasy Mediterranean Fish Dinner

Prep Time 5 minutes, Cook Time 15 minutes, Servings 4

Ingredients

- 1 Tablespoon butter
- 1 lb of white fish, I used frozen tilapia
- 12 oz jar Aldi artichoke salad or other brand equivalent
- 1/3 cup sundried tomatoes chopped
- 1 cup densely packed fresh baby spinach, chopped
- 1 teaspoon crushed garlic
- 2 Tablespoons capers

Instructions

- Thaw fish if frozen and pat dry.
- Melt the butter in a sauté pan over medium high heat.
- Add fish and brown or 2 minutes on each side.
- Add all the ingredients, over and cook for 5-10 minutes over medium heat.
- Serve over rice, cauliflower rice or eat as is.

Nutritional info per serving : Calories 325 kcal, Points Value: 10

Day 21

BREAKFAST

Greek Couscous Salad

Prep: 15 min. Cook: 5 min. + cooling, 12 servings

Ingredients

- 1 can (14-1/2 ounces) reduced-sodium chicken broth
- 1-3/4 cups uncooked whole wheat couscous (about 11 ounces)
- DRESSING:
- 1/2 cup olive oil
- 1-1/2 teaspoons grated lemon zest
- 1/4 cup lemon juice
- 1 teaspoon adobo seasoning
- 1/4 teaspoon salt

SALAD:

- 1 English cucumber, halved lengthwise and sliced
- 2 cups grape tomatoes, halved
- 1 cup coarsely chopped fresh parsley
- 1 can (6-1/2 ounces) sliced ripe olives, drained
- 4 green onions, chopped
- 1/2 cup crumbled feta cheese

Instructions

- In a large saucepan, bring broth to a boil. Stir in couscous. Remove from heat; let stand, covered, until broth is absorbed, about 5 minutes. Transfer to a large bowl; cool completely.
- Whisk together dressing ingredients. Add cucumber, tomatoes, parsley, olives and green onions to couscous; stir in dressing. Gently stir in cheese. Serve immediately or refrigerate and serve cold.

Nutritional info per serving : 3/4 cup: 335 calories, 18g fat (3g saturated fat), 4mg cholesterol, 637mg sodium, 39g carbohydrate (3g sugars, 7g fiber), 9g protein, Points Value: 18

LUNCH

Easy Mediterranean Fish

Prep: 15 m, Cook: 30 m

Ingredients

- 4 (6 ounce) fillets halibut
- 1 tablespoon Greek seasoning (such as Cavender's®)
- 1 large tomato, chopped
- 1 onion, chopped
- 1 (5 ounce) jar pitted kalamata olives
- 1/4 cup capers
- 1/4 cup olive oil
- 1 tablespoon lemon juice
- salt and pepper to taste

Instructions

- Preheat an oven to 350 degrees F (175 degrees C).
- Place halibut fillets on a large sheet of aluminum foil and season with Greek seasoning. Combine tomato, onion, olives, capers, olive oil, lemon juice, salt, and pepper in a bowl. Spoon tomato mixture over the halibut. Carefully seal all the edges of the foil to create a large packet. Place the packet on a baking sheet.
- Bake in the preheated oven until the fish flakes easily with a fork, 30 to 40 minutes.

Nutritional info per serving : 429 calories; 26.8 g fat; 9.2 g carbohydrates; 36.6 g protein; 54 mg cholesterol; 1275 mg sodium, , Points Value: 19

DINNER

Prawns with Honey Sauce

Prep/Cook Time: 20 minutes, Servings 1-2

Ingredients:

- 4 large prawns
- 1 glass wine of unripe grape
- or 1 glass of lemon juice and 1/2 white wine
- 1/2 tbs brown fennel seeds
- 1 sour apple grated
- 3 tbs honey
- 1 tsp niggela seeds
- a little olive oil

Instructions:

- Sauté the prawns in the oil and once they are half done add the fennel seeds and then the apple.
- Immediately douse the prawns with the juice.
- Leave it until the liquids are half drained and add the honey.
- When the sauce thickens serve and if you like sprinkle with some niggela seeds.

★★WW Salad, Soup & Snacks★★

Balsamic Cucumber Salad

Prep/Cook Time: 15 min, 6 servings

Ingredients

- 1 large English cucumber, halved and sliced
- 2 cups grape tomatoes, halved
- 1 medium red onion, halved and thinly sliced
- 1/2 cup balsamic vinaigrette
- 3/4 cup crumbled reduced-fat feta cheese

Instructions

- In a large bowl, combine cucumber, tomatoes and onion. Add vinaigrette; toss to coat. Refrigerate, covered, until serving. Just before serving, stir in cheese. Serve with a slotted spoon.

Nutritional info per serving : 3/4 cup: 90 calories, 5g fat (1g saturated fat), 5mg cholesterol, 356mg sodium, 9g carbohydrate (5g sugars, 1g fiber), 4g protein, Points Value: 3

Mediterranean Chicken Orzo Soup

Prep: 20 min. Cook: 25 min, 6 servings (2-1/2 quarts)

Ingredients

- 2 tablespoons olive oil, divided
- 3/4 pound boneless skinless chicken breasts, cubed
- 2 celery ribs, chopped
- 2 medium carrots, chopped
- 1 small onion, chopped
- 1/2 teaspoon salt

- 1/2 teaspoon dried oregano
- 1/4 teaspoon pepper
- 1/4 cup white wine or additional reduced-sodium chicken broth
- 1 carton (32 ounces) reduced-sodium chicken broth
- 1 teaspoon minced fresh rosemary
- 1 bay leaf
- 1 cup uncooked whole wheat orzo pasta
- 1 teaspoon grated lemon zest
- 1 tablespoon lemon juice
- Minced fresh parsley, optional

Instructions

- In a large saucepan, heat 1 tablespoon oil over medium-high heat. Add chicken; cook and stir 6-8 minutes or until no longer pink. Remove from pan.
- In same pan, heat remaining oil over medium-high heat. Add vegetables, salt, oregano and pepper; cook and stir 4-6 minutes or until vegetables are crisp-tender. Add wine, stirring to loosen browned bits from pan. Stir in broth, rosemary and bay leaf; bring to a boil.
- Add orzo. Reduce heat; simmer, covered, 15-18 minutes or until orzo is tender, stirring occasionally. Return chicken to pan; heat through. Stir in lemon zest and juice; remove bay leaf. If desired, top each serving with parsley.

Nutritional info per serving : 1-2/3 cups: 223 calories, 6g fat (1g saturated fat), 31mg cholesterol, 630mg sodium, 23g carbohydrate (2g sugars, 5g fiber), 17g protein, Points Value: 8

Mediterranean Shrimp Orzo Salad

Prep/Total Time: 30 min, 8 servings

Ingredients

- 1 package (16 ounces) orzo pasta
- 3/4 pound peeled and deveined cooked shrimp (31-40 per pound), cut into thirds
- 1 can (14 ounces) water-packed quartered artichoke hearts, rinsed and drained
- 1 cup finely chopped green pepper

- 1 cup finely chopped sweet red pepper
- 3/4 cup finely chopped red onion
- 1/2 cup pitted Greek olives
- 1/2 cup minced fresh parsley
- 1/3 cup chopped fresh dill
- 3/4 cup Greek vinaigrette

Instructions

- Cook orzo according to package Instructions. Drain; rinse with cold water and drain well.
- In a large bowl, combine orzo, shrimp, vegetables, olives and herbs. Add vinaigrette; toss to coat. Refrigerate, covered, until serving.

Nutritional info per serving : 1-1/2 cups: 397 calories, 12g fat (2g saturated fat), 65mg cholesterol, 574mg sodium, 52g carbohydrate (4g sugars, 3g fiber), 18g protein, Points Value: 20

Favorite Mediterranean Salad

Prep/Total Time: 20 min, 28 servings (3/4 cup each)

Ingredients

- 18 cups torn romaine (about 2 large bunches)
- 1 medium cucumber, sliced
- 1 cup crumbled feta cheese
- 1 cup cherry tomatoes, quartered
- 1 small red onion, thinly sliced
- 1/2 cup julienned roasted sweet red peppers
- 1/2 cup pitted Greek olives, halved

DRESSING:

- 2/3 cup olive oil
- 1/4 cup red wine vinegar
- 1 garlic clove, minced
- 1 teaspoon Italian seasoning
- 1/4 teaspoon salt
- 1/4 teaspoon pepper

Instructions

- In a very large salad bowl, combine the first seven ingredients. In a small bowl, whisk the dressing ingredients. Drizzle over salad and toss to coat.

Nutritional info per serving : 3/4 cup: 69 calories, 6g fat (1g saturated fat), 2mg cholesterol, 117mg sodium, 2g carbohydrate (1g sugars, 1g fiber), 1g protein, Points Value: 4

Greek Spring Soup

Prep Time :10 mins, Cook Time: 25 mins, Servings: 4 -6

Ingredients

- 6 cups chicken broth homemade or canned
- 1 1/2 cups diced or shredded cooked chicken
- 2 Tablespoons olive oil
- 1 small onion diced about 3/4 cup
- 1 bay leaf
- 1/3 cup arborio rice
- 1 large eggs
- Juice of half of a lemon
- 1 cup chopped asparagus
- 1 cup diced carrots
- 1/2 cup of fresh chopped dill divided
- Kosher salt and fresh pepper to taste
- Fresh minced chives for garnish

Instructions

- In a large stock pot, heat 2 tablespoons olive oil over medium heat. Sauté onions until soft and translucent, about 5 minutes. Add 1/4 cup dill, chicken broth, bay leaf and bring to a boil.
- Add rice and reduce heat to medium low, and simmer about 10 minutes. Add carrots and asparagus and cook an additional 10-15 minutes, or until rice is cooked and vegetables are tender. Add chicken and continue to simmer on low while preparing egg and lemon juice mixture.
- Meanwhile, in a separate bowl, combine egg, lemon juice and 2 tablespoons of water.
- Slowly whisk about half a cup of the hot stock into the egg mixture, stirring constantly, to keep eggs from curdling.
- Slowly whisk the egg/lemon broth back into the stock pot. Soup will thicken slightly. Turn off heat and remove bay leaf.
- Add remaining fresh dill, and adjust seasoning with salt and pepper.

Roasted Red Pepper and Tomato Soup

Prep Time: 10 mins, Cook Time: 45 mins, Servings: 4 cups

Ingredients

- 2 red bell peppers, seeded and halved
- 3 tomatoes, cored and halved
- 1/2 medium onion, quartered
- 2 cloves garlic, peeled and halved
- 1-2 tablespoon olive oil
- 1/4 teaspoon salt
- 1/4 teaspoon ground black pepper
- 2 cups vegetable broth
- 2 tablespoons tomato paste
- 1/4 cup fresh parsley, chopped
- 1/4 teaspoon Italian seasoning blend
- 1/4 teaspoon ground paprika
- 1/8 teaspoon. ground cayenne pepper, or more to taste

Instructions

- Preheat oven to 375 F. Place red pepper, tomatoes, onion and garlic on a baking tray. Toss with olive oil, salt and pepper. Arrange the tomatoes and bell peppers with the cut-side up. Bake for 45 minutes, until vegetables are tender.
- In a medium saucepan, heat the vegetable broth on medium heat. Add the roasted vegetables (reserve half a red bell pepper for garnish), tomato paste, parsley, paprika and cayenne pepper. Stir to combine. Simmer for ten minutes.
- In a food processor or blender, purée the soup and transfer back into the pot. Cook on low heat for another 5 minutes. If you desire a thicker consistency, cook a few minutes longer. Add salt and pepper, to taste.
- Pour the soup into a bowl and garnish with the reserved roasted red pepper. Serve with crackers.

Greek Lemon Chicken Soup

Prep Time 10 mins, Cook Time 20 mins, Servings: 8

Ingredients

- 10 cups chicken broth
- 3 tablespoon olive oil
- 8 cloves garlic, minced
- 1 sweet onion
- 1 large lemon, zested
- 2 boneless skinless chicken breasts
- 1 cup israeli (pearl) couscous
- 1/2 teaspoons crushed red pepper
- 2 ounces crumbled feta
- 1/3 cup chopped chive
- Salt and pepper

Instructions

- Place the olive oil in a large 6-8 quart sauce pot over medium-low heat. Peel the onion. Then quarter it and slice into thin strips. Once the oil is hot, saute the onion and minced garlic for 3-4 minutes to soften.
- Add the chicken broth, raw chicken breasts, lemon zest, and crushed red pepper to the pot. Raise the heat to high, cover, and bring to a boil. Once boiling, reduce the heat to medium, then simmer for 5 minutes.
- Stir in the couscous, 1 teaspoon salt, and black pepper to taste. Simmer another 5 minutes. Then turn the heat off.
- Using tongs, remove the two chicken breasts from the pot. Use a fork and the tongs to shred the chicken. Then place it back in the pot. Stir in the crumbled feta cheese and chopped chive. Taste and salt and pepper as needed. Serve warm.

Nutritional info per serving : Calories 286 , Calories from Fat 99 , Total Fat 11g 17% , Protein 15g 30%, Points Value: 10

Dad's Greek Salad

Prep/Total Time: 20 min, 8 servings

Ingredients

- 4 large tomatoes, seeded and coarsely chopped
- 2-1/2 cups thinly sliced English cucumbers
- 1 small red onion, halved and thinly sliced
- 1/4 cup olive oil
- 3 tablespoons red wine vinegar
- 1/4 teaspoon salt
- 1/8 teaspoon pepper
- 1/4 teaspoon dried oregano, optional
- 3/4 cup pitted Greek olives
- 3/4 cup crumbled feta cheese

Instructions : Place tomatoes, cucumbers and onion in a large bowl. In a small bowl, whisk oil, vinegar, salt and pepper and, if desired, oregano until blended. Drizzle over salad; toss to coat. Top with olives and cheese.

Nutritional info per serving : 3/4 cup: 148 calories, 12g fat (2g saturated fat), 6mg cholesterol, 389mg sodium, 7g carbohydrate (3g sugars, 2g fiber), 3g protein, Points Value: 7

15 Minute Mediterranean Chickpea Salad

Prep time: 15 mins, Serves: 4

Ingredients

- 1 (15 oz) can chickpeas (drained, rinsed and loose shells removed)
- 1 pint cherry tomatoes, halved
- ½ cucumber, finely chopped
- ¼ cup sliced black olives
- ¼ cup herbed feta (or plain)
- Juice of 1 lemon
- 2 tbsp extra virgin olive oil
- 1 tbsp red wine vinegar
- ¼ cup fresh parsley, finely chopped
- 3 tbsp fresh basil, finely chopped
- ¼ tsp garlic powder
- Pinch of sea salt and black pepper

Instructions : Combine everything in a large bowl, toss to combine, SERVE!

Nutritional info per serving : Serving size: ¼th of recipe Calories: 196 Fat: 11 gm Saturated fat: 1.5 gm Carbohydrates: 22 gm Sugar: 5 gm Sodium: 280 mg Fiber: 5 gm Protein: 7 gm Cholesterol: 5 mg, Points Value: 10

Loaded Mediterranean Hummus

Prep Time: 5 mins, Cook Time: 25 mins, Serving: 4-6

Ingredients

For the hummus:

- 1 can chickpeas
- 2 tbsp tahini
- 3 tbsp olive oil
- 1 garlic clove
- 1 tsp lemon juice
- 1/2 tsp paprika
- 1/4 tsp cumin
- 4 tbsp water
- 1 tbsp packed fresh cilantro
- salt and pepper to taste

For the toppings:

- 1/4 cup crispy chickpeas
- 1/4 cup cherry tomatoes
- 1/4 cup red onion
- 1/4 cup cucumber
- sesame seeds (optional)

- fresh cilantro

Instructions

- To make crispy chickpeas, preheat oven to 400 degrees. Drizzle canned chickpeas with olive oil and bake for about 25 minutes (until crispy).
- Combine all hummus ingredients in a food processor and blend to desired consistency.
- Cut tomatoes, cucumber, and red onion into small pieces and place on top of the hummus. Top with chickpeas, sesame seeds and fresh cilantro.

Nutritional info per serving : Calories 69.9 ,Calories from Fat 36 (51.5%) , Total Fat 4g , Saturated fat 0.5g , Sodium 80.1mg 4% , Carbohydrates 6g, Points Value: 3

Crock Pot Chunky Monkey Paleo Trail Mix

Prep Time: 5 min, Cook Time: 1 hr, 30 min. Serving: 5-6 cups

Ingredients

- 2 cup raw walnuts (halves or coarsely chopped)
- 1 cup raw cashews halves or whole almonds work too)
- 1 cup unsweetened coconut flakes (be sure to get big FLAKES not shredded)
- 1/3 cup coconut sugar
- 1.5 tbsp butter (cut in slices) or at room temp 2 to 3 tbsp coconut oil to make vegan
- 1 tsp vanilla or butter extract
- 6 ounces unsweetened banana chips or dried banana slices
- 1/2 cup to 2/3 cup dark chocolate chips or paleo fudge chunks (we used Enjoy life foods brand)

Instructions

- Place your nuts, coconut, sugar, vanilla, and butter slices or coconut oil in a crock pot. Mix together and place on high for 45- 60 minutes. Stir a few times checking to make sure coconut flakes do not burn. NOTE - Reduce to low after 45 minutes if flakes are cooking faster or browning.
- Turn to low and continue cooking for 20-30 minutes.

- o Remove and place crock pot contents on parchment paper to dry out. Be sure to let it cool for at least 15 minutes before adding the chocolate and banana chips.
- o Add in the banana chips and chocolate chips and mix together.
- o OPTION – cooking banana chips – You can add in your unsweetened banana chips to cook with the nuts/coconut, instead of adding later. But you will need to stir often and cook only 45 minutes.
- o Store in an airtight container or ziplock bag

Notes

- For vegans – If you are using coconut oil, use 3 tbsp to start and then adjust halfway to make sure all ingredients dissolve. You might need more or less.
- To lighten up the sugar/calories, use Stevia baking sugar and 1/2 cup of dark chocolate.

Nutritional info per serving : Serving Size: 1/4 cup Calories: 250 Sugar: 12.5g Carbohydrates: 18.6g Fiber: 3.5g Protein: 4g, Points Value: 10

Peanut Butter Banana Greek Yogurt Bowl

Prep/Cook Time: 5 minutes, Servings:4

Ingredients

- 4 cups vanilla Greek yogurt
- 2 medium bananas sliced
- 1/4 cup creamy natural peanut butter
- 1/4 cup flax seed meal
- 1 teaspoon nutmeg

Instructions

- o Divide yogurt between four bowls and top with banana slices.
- o Melt peanut butter in a microwave safe bowl for 30-40 seconds and drizzle one tablespoon on each bowl on top of the bananas.
- o Sprinkle with flax seed meal and ground nutmeg to serve.

Nutritional info per serving : Calories 370 , Calories from Fat 95 , Total Fat 10.6g 16%, Points Value: 14

Lemon Chicken Orzo Soup

Prep Time: 10 mins, Cook Time: 20 mins, Servings : 6

Ingredients:

- 2 tablespoons olive oil, divided
- 1 pound boneless, skinless chicken thighs, cut into 1-inch chunks
- Kosher salt and freshly ground black pepper
- 3 cloves garlic, minced
- 1 onion, diced
- 3 carrots, peeled and diced
- 2 stalks celery, diced
- 1/2 teaspoon dried thyme
- 5 cups chicken stock
- 2 bay leaves
- 3/4 cup uncooked orzo pasta
- 1 sprig rosemary
- Juice of 1 lemon
- 2 tablespoons chopped fresh parsley leaves

Instructions:

- Heat 1 tablespoon olive oil in a large stockpot or Dutch oven over medium heat. Season chicken thighs with salt and pepper, to taste. Add chicken to the stockpot and cook until golden, about 2-3 minutes; set aside.
- Add remaining 1 tablespoon oil to the stockpot. Add garlic, onion, carrots and celery. Cook, stirring occasionally, until tender, about 3-4 minutes. Stir in thyme until fragrant, about 1 minute.
- Whisk in chicken stock, bay leaves and 1 cup water; bring to a boil. Stir in orzo, rosemary and chicken; reduce heat and simmer until orzo is tender, about 10-12 minutes. Stir in lemon juice and parsley; season with salt and pepper, to taste.
- Serve immediately.

Nutritional info per serving : Calories 300.8 Calories from Fat 106.2 , Total Fat 11.8g 18% , Saturated Fat 2.6g 13% , Trans Fat 0g , Cholesterol 68.5mg 23% , Sodium 377.8mg 16%, Points Value: 12

Smoky Loaded Eggplant Dip: Baba Ganoush

Prep Time: 15 mins, Cook Time: 20 min, Servings: Serves 4-6

Ingredients

For Smoky Eggplant Dip (Baba Ganoush)

- 1 large eggplant
- 2 tbsp tahini paste
- 1 1/2 tbsp Greek yogurt
- 1 garlic clove, chopped
- 1 tbsp lemon juice
- Salt and pepper
- 1 tsp sumac, more for garnish
- 3/4 tsp Aleppo pepper
- 1/ tsp crushed red pepper (optional)
- Toasted pine nuts for garnish

For Salad Topping

- 1 Tomato, diced
- 1/2 English Cucumber, diced
- Large handful fresh parsley
- Salt and Pepper
- 1/2 tsp sumac
- Splash fresh lemon juice
- Drizzle Early Harvest extra virgin olive oil

Instructions

- Make the salad topping. In a bowl add tomato, cucumber, and parsley. Season with salt, pepper, and sumac. Add lemon juice and a generous drizzle of extra virgin olive oil. Toss and set aside.
- Smoke Eggplant: Turn 1 gas burner on high. Using a pair of tongs, turn eggplant every 5 minutes or so until the eggplant is completely tender and it's skin is charred and crispy (about 15 to 20 minutes.) Don't worry if the eggplant deflates, it's supposed to. (You can also do this on a gas or charcoal grill over medium-high heat.) Remove from heat and let the eggplant cool.
- Remove Eggplant Skin & Drain Excess Water. Once eggplant is cool enough to touch, peel the charred crispy skin off. Discard the stem. Transfer eggplant flesh to a colander; let drain for 3 minutes.
- Blend the Dip. Transfer eggplant flesh to the bowl of a food processor. Add tahini paste, yogurt, garlic, lemon juice, salt, pepper, Sumac, Aleppo pepper, crushed red pepper (if using.) Give it just a couple of pulses to combine (do not over blend. See notes)
- Transfer the smoky eggplant dip (baba ganoush) to a serving bowl. Cover and refrigerate for 30 minutes (or overnight).
- Bring eggplant dip to room temperature. Top with a generous drizzle of extra virgin olive oil. Add pine nuts. Spoon the salad on top (be sure to drain any excess liquid before adding on top of the baba ganoush.) Serve with warm pita wedges or pita chips.

Savory Feta Spinach and Sweet Red Pepper Muffins

Prep Time: 10 mins, Cook Time: 25 mins, Servings: 12

Ingredients

- 2 ¾ cups all purpose flour (you can substitute partly with whole wheat flour)
- ¼ cup sugar
- 2 teaspoons baking powder
- 1 teaspoon paprika
- ¾ teaspoon salt
- ¾ cup low fat milk
- ½ cup extra virgin olive oil
- 2 eggs
- 1 ¼ cup thinly sliced fresh spinach
- ¾ cup crumbled feta
- 1/3 cup drained and patted dry jarred Florina peppers or other red pepper

Instructions

- Preheat oven at 375 F (190 C).
- In a large bowl mix the dry ingredients: flour, sugar, baking powder, paprika, and salt)
- In another bowl mix the olive oil, eggs, milk.
- Add the wet ingredients to the dry ingredients and mix just until blended with a wooden spoon. The dough will be thick.
- Add the feta, spinach and peppers and mix gently until all ingredients are spread throughout the whole mixture.
- Divide mixture in muffin pan that you have lined with muffin/cupcake liners or you can use a silicon muffin tray and grease it with a bit of olive oil (I have used it here). You should have enough for 12 medium muffins.
- Bake for about 25 minutes. Remove when toothpick comes out clear when inserted in the muffin.
- Let them cool for 10 minutes and remove from tray. Let them cool a couple of hours before serving.

Nutritional info per serving : Calories per serving: 240, Points Value: 7

Mediterranean Roasted Chickpeas Recipe

Prep Time 5 mins, Cook Time 30 mins, Servings 2

Ingredients

- 2 15 oz Cans Chickpeas
- 2 Tbsp Extra Virgin Olive Oil
- 2 tsp Red Wine Vinegar
- 2 tsp Fresh Lemon Juice
- 1 tsp Kosher Salt
- 1 tsp Dried Oregano
- 1/2 tsp Garlic Powder
- 1/2 tsp Cracked Black Pepper

Instructions

- Preheat oven to 425 degrees and line a baking sheet with parchment paper. Drain, rinse, and thoroughly dry the chickpeas, then place in a single layer on the baking sheet.
- Roast for 10 minutes, then remove from oven, use a spatula to turn the chickpeas so they bake evenly, then roast for another 10 minutes.
- In a large mixing bowl, add the remaining ingredients and whisk to combine. Add the hot chickpeas and toss gently until fully coated.
- Place the coated chickpeas back onto the baking sheet and continue roasting for 10 more minutes, checking occasionally to be ensure they don't overcook and burn. Allow to cool completely and enjoy!

Nutritional info per serving : Calories 111 , Calories from Fat 29 , Total Fat 3.2g 5% , Saturated Fat 0.3g 2% , Sodium 175.2mg 7% , Total Carbohydrates 16.3g 5%, Points Value: 12 , Points Value: 4

Mediterranean Cobb Salad

Prep: 1 hour Cook: 5 min./batch, 10 servings

Ingredients

- 1 package (6 ounces) falafel mix
- 1/2 cup sour cream or plain yogurt
- 1/4 cup chopped seeded peeled cucumber
- 1/4 cup 2% milk
- 1 teaspoon minced fresh parsley
- 1/4 teaspoon salt
- 4 cups torn romaine
- 4 cups fresh baby spinach
- 3 hard-boiled large eggs, chopped
- 2 medium tomatoes, seeded and finely chopped
- 1 medium ripe avocado, peeled and finely chopped

- 3/4 cup crumbled feta cheese
- 8 bacon strips, cooked and crumbled
- 1/2 cup pitted Greek olives, finely chopped

Instructions

- Prepare and cook falafel according to package Instructions. When cool enough to handle, crumble or coarsely chop falafel.
- In a small bowl, mix sour cream, cucumber, milk, parsley and salt. In a large bowl, combine romaine and spinach; transfer to a platter. Arrange crumbled falafel and remaining ingredients over greens. Drizzle with dressing.

Nutritional info per serving : 1 cup: 258 calories, 18g fat (5g saturated fat), 83mg cholesterol, 687mg sodium, 15g carbohydrate (3g sugars, 5g fiber), 13g protein,
Points Value: 11

Quinoa Tabbouleh Salad

Prep: 15 min. Cook: 15 min. + cooling, 6 servings

Ingredients

- 2 cups water
- 1 cup quinoa, rinsed
- 3/4 cup packed fresh parsley sprigs, stems removed
- 1/3 cup fresh mint leaves
- 1/4 cup coarsely chopped red onion
- 1 garlic clove, minced
- 1 cup grape tomatoes
- 1/2 English cucumber, cut into 1-inch pieces
- 2 tablespoons lemon juice
- 2 tablespoons olive oil
- 1 teaspoon salt
- 1/2 teaspoon pepper
- 1/4 teaspoon ground allspice

Instructions

- In a large saucepan, bring water to a boil. Add quinoa. Reduce heat; simmer, covered, 12-15 minutes or until liquid is absorbed. Remove from heat; fluff with a fork. Transfer to a large bowl; cool completely.
- Place parsley, mint, onion and garlic in a food processor; pulse until finely chopped. Add tomatoes and cucumber; pulse until coarsely chopped. Add tomato mixture to quinoa.
- In a small bowl, whisk lemon juice, oil and seasonings until blended; drizzle over quinoa mixture and toss to coat. Serve at room temperature or refrigerate until serving.

Nutritional info per serving : 2/3 cup: 163 calories, 6g fat (1g saturated fat), 0 cholesterol, 403mg sodium, 22g carbohydrate (2g sugars, 3g fiber), 5g protein, Points Value: 8

Easy Moroccan Chickpea Stew

Prep/Total Time: 30 min, 4 servings

Ingredients

- 1 tablespoon olive oil
- 2 cups cubed peeled butternut squash (1/2-inch cubes)
- 1 large onion, chopped
- 1 large sweet red pepper, chopped
- 1 teaspoon ground cinnamon
- 1/2 teaspoon pepper
- 1/4 teaspoon ground ginger
- 1/4 teaspoon ground cumin
- 1/4 teaspoon salt
- 1 can (15 ounces) chickpeas or garbanzo beans, rinsed and drained
- 1 can (14-1/2 ounces) diced tomatoes, undrained
- 1 cup water
- Chopped cilantro, optional

Instructions

- In a Dutch oven, heat oil over medium-high heat. Add squash, onion and red pepper; cook and stir until onion is translucent and red pepper is crisp-tender, about 5 minutes. Stir in seasonings until blended.
- Add remaining ingredients; bring to a boil. Reduce heat; cover and simmer until squash is tender, about 8 minutes. If desired, top with cilantro.

Nutritional info per serving : 1-1/2 cups: 217 calories, 6g fat (1g saturated fat), 0 cholesterol, 455mg sodium, 38g carbohydrate (11g sugars, 9g fiber), 7g protein, Points Value: 11

★★ WW Fish & Sea food ★★

Mediterranean Seafood Stew

Prep/Total Time: 30 min, 6 servings

Ingredients

- 1 medium onion, finely chopped
- 1 tablespoon olive oil
- 1-1/2 teaspoons minced garlic, divided
- 1/2 pound plum tomatoes, seeded and diced
- 1 teaspoon grated lemon peel
- 1/4 teaspoon crushed red pepper flakes
- 1 cup clam juice
- 1/3 cup white wine or additional clam juice
- 1 tablespoon tomato paste
- 1/2 teaspoon salt
- 1 pound orange roughy or red snapper fillets, cut into 1-inch cubes
- 1 pound uncooked large shrimp, peeled and deveined
- 1/2 pound sea scallops
- 1/3 cup minced fresh parsley
- 1/3 cup reduced-fat mayonnaise

Instructions

- In a Dutch oven, saute onion in oil until tender. Add 1/2 teaspoon garlic; cook 1 minute longer. Add the tomatoes, lemon peel and pepper flakes; cook and stir for 2 minutes. Add the clam juice, wine or additional clam juice, tomato paste and salt. Bring to a boil. Reduce heat; cover and simmer for 10 minutes or until heated through.
- Add the fish, shrimp, scallops and parsley. Cover and cook for 8-10 minutes or until fish flakes easily with a fork, the shrimp turn pink and scallops are opaque. Combine mayonnaise and remaining garlic; dollop onto each serving.

Nutritional info per serving : 1 cup: 221 calories, 8g fat (1g saturated fat), 123mg cholesterol, 607mg sodium, 7g carbohydrate (0 sugars, 1g fiber), 28g protein, Points Value: 7

Mediterranean Seafood Sauté with Garlic Couscous

Prep Time: 5 mins, Cook Time: 10 mins, 6 Servings

Ingredients

- 1 lb. codfish, cut into 1-inch pieces
- 1/2 lb. raw shrimp, peeled, deveined, and coarsely chopped
- 1/2 lb. bay scallops
- 4 scallions, sliced
- 1/2 cup chopped fresh chives
- 1/2 cup chopped fresh parsley
- Salt and freshly ground pepper to taste
- 2 Tbs. olive oil
- Hot sauce to taste (optional)
- 2 (5.4-oz.) boxes garlic-flavored couscous

Instructions

- In large bowl, combine codfish, shrimp, scallops, scallions, chives, parsley, and salt and pepper to taste. Mix ingredients using large spoon.
- Heat olive oil in large skillet over medium heat. Add fish mixture, and cook, stirring often, until fish is cooked through and lightly browned. Sprinkle with hot sauce, if desired. Reduce heat to very low, and cover to keep warm.
- Prepare couscous according to package instructions. Divide fish into 6 portions, and serve over couscous.

Nutritional info per serving : Calories: 370 , Carbohydrate Content: 43 g , Cholesterol Content: 90 mg , Fat Content: 10 g , Fiber Content: 3 g , Points Value: 19

Zarzuela de Pescado

Prep Time: 10 min, Cook Time 35 min, Serves: 2

Ingredients

- 2 Cloves of Garlic
- 1 Onion
- 1/2 Red Bell Pepper
- 1 1/2 Cups of Tinned Diced Tomatoes
- 1 Tube of Squid
- 1 Fillet of Hake (can be substituted for Halibut/Seabass/Tilapia)
- 10 Jumbo Shrimp (peeled and deveined)
- 8 Fresh Mussels
- 1 Tsp Dried Thyme

- 1 Tsp Smoked Paprika
- 1 Pinch of Saffron in Powder Form
- 1/2 Tsp White Sugar
- 1 1/2 Cups Fish Broth
- 1/4 Cup Water
- 10 Blanched Almonds
- 4 Tbsp Extra Virgin Spanish Olive Oil
- Sea Salt
- Fresh Parsley

Instructions

- Finely mince 2 cloves of garlic, finely dice 1 onion, finely dice 1/2 of a red bell pepper, cut a cleaned tube of squid into small squares and chop a fillet of hake into 6 pieces
- Heat a large non-stick frying pan with a medium heat and add 3 tablespoons of extra virgin Spanish olive oil to the pan
- Once the oil get´s hot, season it with sea salt and add the squid squares, cook for about 2 minutes, remove from the pan and set aside
- Add the diced onion to the pan and cook for about 3 minutes, then add the 2 minced garlics and cook for about 30 seconds, add the diced bell pepper and mix everything together and cook for about 3 minutes
- Add 1 teaspoon of dried thyme, 1 teaspoon of smoked paprika, a pinch of sea salt and mix everything together
- Next add 1 1/2 cups of tinned diced tomatoes, a pinch of white sugar, a pinch of sea salt and mix everything together
- After cooking the tomatoes for 5 minutes, add 1 1/2 cups of fish broth to the pan, 1/2 cup of water, a pinch of saffron in powder form and gently mix all the ingredients in the pan and turn up the heat to a medium-high
- Once it begins to boil, lower the heat to a LOW heat
- Grab a small non-stick frying pan and dry roast 10 blanched almonds for about 4 minutes, then add to a mortar along with 2 tablespoons of fresh parsley and mash together until you form a paste, then add 1 tablespoon of extra virgin Spanish olive oil, mix well and add the mixture to the pan with the rest of the ingredients and mix
- After about 10 minutes, add the 6 pieces of hake to the pan, add the cooked squid you set aside, about 10 jumbo shrimp, 8 fresh mussels and cover the pan
- After about 5 minutes remove the lid and all the mussels should be open and the fish perfectly cooked, remove from the heat
- Garnish with some fresh parsley and serve straight from the pan
- Enjoy!

Nutritional info per serving : Serving size: 1 large bowl , Calories: 554 , Fat: 29 , Trans fat: 0 , Carbohydrates: 21, Points Value: 22

Mediterranean Fish (Flounder)

Prep/Cook Time: 40 mins, SERVES: 4

Ingredients

- 5 roma tomatoes, chopped or 1 (15 ounce) can chopped tomatoes
- 2 tablespoons olive oil
- 1/2 onion, chopped
- 2 garlic cloves, chopped
- 1 pinch italian seasoning
- 1/4 cup white wine
- 24 kalamata olives, pitted and chopped
- 4 tablespoons capers
- 1 teaspoon lemon juice, fresh perfered
- 6 leaves fresh basil, chopped
- 3 tablespoons parmesan cheese
- 1 lb flounder (any firm fish) or 1 lb sole (any firm fish) or 1 lb halibut (any firm fish) or 1 lb mahi mahi (any firm fish) or 1 lb tilapia fillet (any firm fish)

Instructions

- Preheat oven to 425 degrees.
- Prepare tomatoes if using fresh by plunging them into boiling water, imediately removing them to a bowl of ice water and peeling the skins. Or you can chop them with the skins on or use canned- it is a person preference thing.
- heat olive oil in a medium skillet over medium heat. Add onions and saute until tender. Add garlic and Italian seasoning, stirring to combine. Add tomatoes and cook until tender. Mix in wine, olives, capers, lemon juice and half of the basil. If fresh basil- if fresh basil is not available add a couple teaspoons of dried basil-fresh is always better though. Reduce heat, blend in Parmesan cheese and cook until the mixture is hot and bubbly. If you prefer a thick sauce you can cook until the sauce has reduced to a thick sauce, about 15 minutes.
- Place fish in a shallow baking dish. Cover with the sauce mixture and bake in preheated oven 15-20 minutes depending on the fish used. Fish should flake easily with a fork when done, except for the mahi mahi which flakes when done, just not easily.

Nutritional info per serving : Serving size: 3 ounces , Calories: 99 , Protein: 21 g , Fat: 1 g , Saturated: 0 g, Points Value: 4

Easy Mediterranean Fish Skillet

Prep Time: 15 mins, Cook Time: 15 mins, Servings: 4

Ingredients

- 4 6 ounce fish fillets mahi, cod, halibut or any other firm white fish
- 2 tablespoons olive oil
- 1 medium red pepper, sliced
- 1/2 large onion, sliced
- 4 large garlic cloves, chopped
- 1 teaspoon dried basil
- 1/4 cup chicken stock
- 1/4 cup white wine or chicken stock if on a specific eating plan
- 1/2 cup cherry tomatoes, halved
- 1/3 cup kalamata olives, pitted
- salt and pepper
- Garnish with feta, chopped basil or fresh parsley if desired

Instructions

- Pat fish dry with paper towel. Sprinkle liberally with salt and pepper. Slice vegetables and set aside.
- Heat large cast iron or non stick skillet to medium high heat. Add olive oil and heat for about 30 seconds or until shimmery but not smoking.
- Add fish to hot skillet. DO NOT TOUCH. Sear for 3-4 minutes on each side. When the fish releases from the pan easily it is ready to flip.
- Remove fish from skillet and set aside.
- Add peppers and onion to skillet. Cook 2-3 minutes until slightly soft. Add garlic and tomatoes. Season with salt and pepper.
- Add basil, white wine and chicken stock to vegetables in pan, scraping up all the little bits from the bottom.
- Add fish back to skillet and continue to cook until cooked through and fish flakes easily. Another 3-4 minutes. Toss kalamata's into the pan until slightly heated.
- Serve with a sprinkle of feta, fresh basil or fresh parsley and lemon wedges if desired.

Nutritional info per serving : Calories 253 , Calories from Fat 72 , Total Fat 8g 12% , Saturated Fat 2g 10% , Cholesterol 85mg 28%, Points Value: 10

Mediterranean Baked Fish

Prep/Total Time: 30 min, 4 servings

Ingredients

- 1 cup thinly sliced leeks (white portion only)
- 2 garlic cloves, minced
- 2 teaspoons olive oil
- 12 large fresh basil leaves
- 1-1/2 pounds orange roughy fillets
- 1 teaspoon salt
- 2 plum tomatoes, sliced
- 1 can (2-1/4 ounces) sliced ripe olives, drained
- 1 medium lemon
- 1/8 teaspoon pepper
- 4 fresh rosemary sprigs

Instructions

o In a nonstick skillet, saute leeks and garlic in oil until tender; set aside. Coat a 13-in. x 9-in. baking dish with cooking spray. Arrange basil in a single layer in dish; top with fish fillets. Sprinkle with salt. Top with leek mixture.

o Arrange tomatoes and olives over fish. Thinly slice half of the lemon; place over the top. Squeeze juice from remaining lemon over all. Sprinkle with pepper.

o Cover and bake at 425° for 15-20 minutes or until fish flakes easily with a fork. Garnish with rosemary.

Nutritional info per serving : 4-1/2 ounce-weight: 180 calories, 5g fat (1g saturated fat), 34mg cholesterol, 844mg sodium, 7g carbohydrate (3g sugars, 1g fiber), 26g protein , Points Value: 4

Pan-Roasted Fish with Mediterranean Tomato Sauce

Prep/Cook Time: 32 Mins, Serves 4 (serving size: 1 fillet and 1/2 cup sauce)

Ingredients

- 1 1/2 tablespoons olive oil
- 1 1/2 teaspoons butter
- 2 cups chopped seeded plum tomato
- 1 1/2 tablespoons capers

- 1 tablespoon Dijon mustard
- 3 garlic cloves, minced
- 1 1/2 tablespoons chopped fresh flat-leaf parsley
- 1 1/2 tablespoons minced fresh chives 1 tablespoon minced fresh tarragon
- 3/4 teaspoon kosher salt, divided
- 3/4 teaspoon freshly ground black pepper, divided
- 1/4 teaspoon crushed red pepper
- 1 tablespoon canola oil
- 4 (6-ounce) yellowtail snapper fillets, skin on

Instrctions

- Heat olive oil and butter in a medium skillet over medium-high heat. Add tomato to pan; cook 6 minutes, stirring frequently. Stir in capers, Dijon mustard, and minced garlic; bring to a boil. Reduce heat, and simmer 2 minutes or until slightly thickened, stirring occasionally. Remove from heat. Stir in parsley, chives, tarragon, 1/4 teaspoon salt, 1/4 teaspoon black pepper, and red pepper; keep warm.
- Heat canola oil in a large nonstick skillet over medium-high heat. Sprinkle fish with remaining 1/2 teaspoon salt and remaining 1/2 teaspoon black pepper. Add fish to pan, skin side down; cook 3 minutes or until skin is browned. Turn fish over; cook 3 minutes or until desired degree of doneness. Serve fish with the sauce.

Nutritional info per serving : Calories 282 Fat 12.4g Satfat 2.6g Monofat 7g Polyfat 1.8g Protein 36.1g, Points Value: 8

★★WW Dessert★★

Mint Chocolate Chip Ice Cream

Prep/Done Time: 5m, 1-2 servings

Ingredients

- 2 overripe, frozen bananas (Click for banana-free version)
- pinch of salt
- 1/8 tsp pure peppermint extract, or more as desired
- optional pinch spirulina or natural food coloring
- optional 1/2 cup coconut cream or raw cashews, for a richer taste
- 2-3 tbsp chocolate chips or sugar free chocolate chips

Instructions

- Be sure to buy pure peppermint extract, not mint or imitation peppermint. Add more extract for a more powerful mint flavor, adding slowly because a little goes a long way. If using the optional nuts, soak them 6 hrs to soften, then drain completely.
- Start with bananas that are turning brown. Peel and cut into pieces, then freeze in an airtight bag or container. To make the ice cream, blend all ingredients until completely smooth. You can add the chocolate before or after blending. Serve immediately in a bowl, or transfer to a container and freeze until firm, then scoop out with an ice cream scoop.

Italian Apple Olive Oil Cake

Prep Time: 20 minutes, Cook Time: 45 minutes, Servings: 1 cake

Ingredients

- 2 large Gala apples, peeled and chopped as finely as possible
- Orange juice to soak apples in
- 3 cups all-purpose flour
- 1/2 tsp ground cinnamon
- 1/2 tsp ground nutmeg
- 1 tsp baking powder
- 1 tsp baking soda
- 1 cup sugar
- 1 cup Private Reserve extra virgin olive oil
- 2 large eggs
- 2/3 cup gold raisins, soaked in warm water for 15 minutes and then drained well

- Confectioner's sugar for dusting

Instructions

- Preheat oven to 350 degrees F.
- Place the chopped apples in a bowl and add orange juice; just enough juice to toss and coat apples so as to prevent browning.
- In a large mixing bowl sift together the flour, cinnamon, nutmeg, baking powder and baking soda. Set aside for now
- In the bowl of a stand mixer fitted with a whisk, add sugar and extra virgin olive oil. Mix on low for 2 minutes until well-combined
- While mixer is on, add the eggs, one at a time, and continue to mix another 2 minutes until mixture increases in volume (it should be thicker but still runny)
- In the large bowl with the dry ingredients, make a well in the middle of the flour mixture. Add the wet mixture (the sugar and olive oil mixture) into the well. Using a wooden spoon, stir until just blended; it will be a thick batter (do not add anything to loosen it).
- Drain raisins (which have been soaking in water) completely; and rid apples of excess juice. Add both raisins and apples to the batter and mix with spoon until well-combined. Again, batter will be fairly thick.
- Line a 9-inch cake pan with parchment paper. Spoon thick batter into the pan, and level the top with the back of your wooden spoon.
- Bake in 350 degrees F for 45 minutes or until an inserted tooth pick or wooden skewer comes out clean.
- Cool completely in pan. When ready, simply lift parchment up to transfer cake into a serving dish. Dust with confectioner's sugar. Alternatively, heat some dark honey to serve on top (those with a sweeter tooth like this option.)

Nutritional info per serving : Serves 12 , Calories 294 , Total Fat 11g 17% , Protein 5.3g 11% , Points Value: 11

Lavender honey ice cream

Prep: 30 mins, Cook: 60 mins, Servings: 6-8

Ingredients

- 33cl of whole milk
- 300g of yogurt
- 10cl of cream
- 20g of honey
- 100g of brown sugar
- 1 tsp of dried lavender

Instructions

- Mix whole milk, cream, sugar, honey and lavender in a bowl.
- Pour the mixture in a pan and heat and stir until the mixture reaches 185°F. Remove from the heat.
- Pour the yogurt into the mixture when the mixture is room temperature.
- Put the mix in the fridge overnight.
- Strain the mixture to remove the lavender.
- Pour the mixture in your ice cream maker (we use the Kitchenaid KICA ice cream maker on low speed for 20/25 minutes then put in the freezer.

Nutritional info per serving : 698 calories; 53.5 g fat; 52.9 g carbohydrates; 7.6 g protein; 278 mg cholesterol; 181 mg sodium, Points Value: 37

Paleo Raspberry Cream Pies (vegan, grain-free, gluten-free, dairy-free)

Prep + Cook Time: 20 min, Servings: 12 mini pies + 2 ramekins

Ingredients : For the crust:

- 1/2 cup (43 grams) unsweetened shredded coconut
- 1 cup (145 grams) roasted cashews (mine were salted)
- 1 1/2 tablespoons maple syrup
- 1 teaspoon vanilla extract
- pinch of salt

For the raspberry filling:

- 1 1/2 cups (218 grams) roasted cashews, soaked for 1 hour1 (mine were salted - there's no sub for the cashews)
- 3/4 cup (168 grams) unrefined coconut oil

- 1/4 cup (60 grams) coconut cream (the top, solid part from a can of full-fat coconut milk that's been refrigerated overnight)
- 1/2 cup + 1 tablespoon maple syrup
- 3 cups (384 grams) fresh raspberries, room temperature (do not use cold raspberries!)2
- 1/4 cup + 2 teaspoons (70 milliliters) freshly squeezed lemon juice
- 2 teaspoons vanilla extract
- pinch of salt

Instructions

- Line a muffin pan with 12 muffin liners. Prepare the crust. Heat a pan over medium-high heat and add the coconut. Stir frequently until nicely toasted. Do not walk away from the pan as the coconut starts to burn very quickly! Pour the coconut into a small bowl and let cool for about 5 minutes. You can skip the toasting step but I think it adds so much flavor to the crust!
- Place all the crust ingredients in a high-powered blender and process at low speed until the mixture starts to clump together. Don't process so long that it becomes pasty. When you pinch some of the mixture between your fingers, it should easily clump together. If it doesn't, add a tiny bit of water and process again until it does.
- Divide the mixture between the liners (17 grams per liner) and use the bottom of a shot glass or your fingers to press the mixture firmly over the bottom of the liners.
- Place the pan in the refrigerator while you prepare the filling.
- In a medium saucepan or pot, mix all the filling ingredients together and warm them over low heat just until they're slightly warm and the coconut cream and oil are melted.
- Wipe out the blender jar using a paper towel and pour the filling mixture in the blender. Blend for about 30-60 seconds at high speed until totally smooth. The mixture should be totally smooth, with the exception of raspberry seeds.
- Pour about 1/4 cup (45 grams) of filling over each crust. Pour the remaining filling in the ramekins or another kind of dish.
- Refrigerate for about 6 hours or until firm. If you're in a hurry, place the pan in the freezer.
- Refrigerate the pies in an airtight container for up to 3 days. If you freeze them overnight, they'll need about 70-80 minutes at room temperature

to defrost or about 1 1/2 - 2 hours in the refrigerator. Once properly defrosted, they should be totally creamy.

Chocolate Avocado Pudding With Hazelnuts And Sea Salt

Prep Time: 5 min, Cook Time: 0 min, 4 servings

Ingredients

- 2 large avocado (chilled)
- 1/2 cup full fat coconut milk
- 1/3 cup raw cacao powder
- 1/3 cup maple syrup
- 2 tsp vanilla extract

TOPPINGS

- hazelnuts roughly chopped
- sea salt

Instructions

- Slice the avocados in half and remove the pit. Scoop out the flesh into a food processor. Add the remaining ingredients and blend until smooth and creamy, scraping down the sides as needed.
- Serve the chocolate avocado pudding with a sprinkle of hazelnuts and sea salt.

Nutritional info per serving : Calories: 295.3 , Total Fat: 20.9g , Saturated Fat: 10.2g , Sodium: 10.3mg , Carbohydrates: 29.1g , Fiber: 7.3g , Sugar: 16.5g , Protein: 3.4g, Points Value: 22

No-Bake Mint Chip Cookies

Prep Time: 20 minutes, Cook Time: 1 hour, Serving: 12

Ingredients

- 2 cups (140g) unsweetened shredded coconut
- 1/2 cup (100g) coconut cream*
- 2 tbsp (40g) maple syrup (**see notes for sugar-free option)
- 1 tsp mint extract
- 1/2 tsp spirulina (I get mine from Thrive Market)
- 1/4 cup (30g) cacao nibs
- 1 cup (180g) chocolate chips, melted***

Instructions

- In a food processor or blender, process the coconut until finely ground (but don't go to long/high speed or it will turn into coconut butter).
- Add the coconut cream, sweetener, mint extract, and spirulina. Process to form a sticky dough.
- Add the cacao nibs, and blend briefly to mix them in.
- Scoop out a heaping tablespoon of dough and shape into a cookie. Repeat until all the batter is used, you should get about 12 cookies. If it won't stick together or is too soft to shape, chill for 10 minutes first.
- Freeze for at least 15 minutes to harden.
- Dip/coat in melted chocolate. Sprinkle with cacao nibs.
- Refrigerate or freeze until firm. In the fridge the center will be soft like a peppermint patty, in the freezer it will be firm like a cookie.
- Enjoy!

Nutritional info per serving : Serving Size: 1 cookie (maple syrup version) , Calories: 209 , ,Sugar: 9g , Fat: 18g , Saturated Fat: 14g , Carbohydrates: 17g , Fiber: 5g , Protein: 2g, , Points Value: 12

Grain-Free Hummingbird Cake

Prep Time: 10 mins, Cook Time: 35 mins, Serving : 16

Ingredients

- 2 medium bananas, overripe and smashed
- 1/4 cup oil (I used avocado oil)
- 1/2 cup honey (or maple syrup)
- 4 eggs
- 3/4 cup crushed pineapple, lightly drained.
- 2 teaspoons gluten-free vanilla extract
- 3 cups Bob's Red Mill Super Fine Almond Flour
- 1/2 teaspoon salt
- 2 teaspoons baking soda
- 4 cups coconut whipped cream (or regular whipped cream) for frosting

Instructions

- Preheat oven to 350°F (180°C). Grease two 8-inch cake pans; set aside.

- Place all ingredients into a large mixing bowl and mix until combined. You don't need to separate the dry and wet ingredients for this recipe.
- Divide batter between the two prepared cake pans. Smooth the top of the batter.
- Bake for 32 - 35 minutes or until the top starts to darken and the center is set. The cakes will be a darker, but golden brown.
- Remove from the oven and let cool for 10 minutes before transferring to a wire rack to cool completely.
- Once cool, frost the tops of the cakes and stack them.
- Store covered in the refrigerator for up to 4 days.

Nutritional info per serving : Calories: 347 , Total Fat: 23g , Saturated Fat: 7g , Trans Fat: 0g , Protein: 7g, Points Value: 19

Maple Vanilla Bean Meringue Cookies

Prep Time: 20 mins, Cook Time: 3 hours

Ingredients

- 2 egg whites (66g), room temperature
- 1/8 tsp cream of tartar
- Pinch of sea salt
- 1/2 cup maple syrup (118mL)
- 1 vanilla bean, scraped

Instructions

- Preheat oven to 200°F (90°C). Line baking sheet with parchment paper.
- Create a double boiler by bringing about an inch of water to a simmer in a medium saucepan.
- In a medium-sized glass or metal mixing bowl that fits over the saucepan without touching the water, whisk together all ingredients.
- Place the bowl on top of the saucepan. While continuously whisking, bring the egg white mixture to 140°F (60°C). If you do not have a candy thermometer, heat the mixture for about 3-5 minutes until it is very warm (use of a candy thermometer is highly recommended though – see note above).
- Remove the bowl from the heat and beat the egg white mixture in the bowl of a stand mixer with a whisk attachment. Begin on a low speed and then gradually increase to high. Beat the mixture for about 8 minutes

- or until the meringue is cool, looks shiny and pearlescent white, and forms stiff peaks.
- Use a very clean silicon spatula or soup spoon to spoon the meringue into a pastry bag fitted with the piping tip of your choice. I use a wide star tip.
- Pipe the meringue into little cookies (about the diameter of a golf ball or smaller) on the parchment paper. They don't really spread much when baking so you don't need too much room between the cookies. Alternately, you can just spoon the meringue onto the parchment paper in little dollops for a freeform, rustic look.
- Bake on the center rack for 2 hours, flipping the baking sheet at the halfway point.
- At the end of the 2 hours, turn off the oven, leave the door closed, and allow the cookies to cool in the oven for at least 1 hour. You can tell when they are done because they will easily come off the parchment paper. If they are stuck at all, leave them in the oven a bit longer.
- After the cookies come to room temperature, store them in an air-tight container.

Vegan Mango Mousse

Prep Time: 10 mins, Cook Time: 50 mins, Servings: 4

Ingredients

- 3 ripe mangoes
- 1 ½ cup coconut cream
- 3 tbsp agave syrup Or 2 tbsp powdered sugar

Instructions

- Peel the mangoes and dice them.
- Mash the dices to make a smooth puree/pulp.
- In a big bowl, gently add the coconut cream and whisk the pulp until it is creamy.
- Add Sugar or Agave syrup.
- Garnish the Mousse with fresh fruits or dark chocolate shavings.
- That's it! Refrigerate them for a few hours and serve chilled for a sweet indulgence!

Nutritional info per serving : Calories 276.9 , Total Fat 0.9 g , Cholesterol 2.2 mg , Sodium 169.7 mg , Potassium 189.3 mg , Points Value: 17

Blackberry Frozen Yogurt

Prep Time: 20 mins: Servings: 6 Servings

Ingredients

- 32 ounces plain Greek yogurt
- 12 ounces fresh blackberries, rinsed
- 1 cup honey, more or less to taste
- a drop or two of pure vanilla extract, if desired

Instructions

- Place the blackberries in the bowl of a food processor. Process until smooth. Strain the blackberries through a fine mesh sieve set over a large mixing bowl. Using the back of a spoon, press the mixture against the sieve to extract all the juice. Discard the seeds and any pulp.
- Add the yogurt to the blackberry juice and stir to combine. Add about 3/4 cup of honey and taste for sweetness. You may need more honey depending on how sweet the blackberries are. I used just under 1 cup. Add vanilla if desired and blend until smooth.
- Process in an ice cream maker according to manufacturer instructions. Serve immediately if you prefer a soft serve consistency or freeze until firm. If frozen remove from the freezer about 15 minutes before serving.

Nutritional info per serving : Calories 104 , Calories from Fat 0 (0%) , Total Fat 0g , Cholesterol 1mg , Sodium 92mg 4% , Carbohydrates 24.2g, Points Value: 10

Conclusion

I hope this book was able to help you lose weight! If you enjoyed this book, would you be kind enough to share this book with your family, friends, and or co-workers and leave a review on Amazon. By you leaving an honest review for this book on Amazon you will help guide people on Amazon to know that this book is legit and perhaps it can help them out as well.

Made in the
USA
Columbia, SC